iPhone

User Manual

For Beginner and Senior to Fully Operate iPhone 11, 11 Pro & 11 Pro Max Using iOS 13 Easily and Become Professional

Ephong Globright

Copyright © 2020

Facts Acclamation

This iPhone User Manual for 11, 11 Pro and 11 Pro Max is primarily designed to provide the complete solutions to several operational challenges on the use of many basic apps, technical setup, ensuring comfortable and safe usage of the iPhone by the dummies, beginners, and senior.

Table of Contents

INTRODUCTION

This is a 3 in 1 User Guide for iPhone 11, 11 Pro and 11 Pro Max that fully explained all the important steps of operating your iPhone effectively according to your needs to enjoy the total benefits of the latest iPhone models from Apple pack to individual setup, uses of apps (apps), creation of important codes, protection of data/document and your iPhone with easier to know tips, techniques and a self-explanatory screenshot of every step.

The major operational steps were in bold words with distinct red color to let you know the separate pages you will navigate through before you can completely activate the operational settings of a particular app's feature on your iPhone.

In some processes, you will see sub-stages that were written in bold words with **black color** while some processes were buttressed with the same bullets to make the progressive steps comprehensive for dummies, beginners, and senor to understand.

For example on **How to make Low Battery Mode in Settings:**

Homescreen: Hit on the **Settings icon.**

Settings: Move down the page to select on **Battery**

Battery: Hit on the **Low Power Mode** activation switch to change to Green.

The red bold words represented the individual pages that you will search through before you can get what you are looking for on the page that was written in black bold words.

The black bold words are the words you are looking for on each page. Except for Homescreen on your iPhone, you will see Settings at the head of the page and you also see Battery at the head of its page.

In this book all the essential icons you must know on your iPhone as a beginner were completely screenshot and labeled for quick recognition. At your relaxing pace, this guide could be read to dig deep into every hint and fact that exposes every hidden secret that ensures the efficient function of your latest iPhone 11, 11 Pro, or 11 Pro Max running with iOS 13.

The recognition of your iPhone starts from the external part of the iPhone and all the important tools on the body that you must familiarize yourself with was initially discussed, to enable you to know everything about your iPhone.

iPhone Properties Clues

iPhone 11 Properties

iPhone 11 working efficiency is enhanced with 4 GB (Gigabyte) of *Apple A13 Biotic Chipset Random Access Memory.*

iPhone internal memories range from 64 GB, 128 GB to 256 GB that responsible for the iPhone price differences.

iPhone 11 is produced with a thickness of 8.33mm or 0.33 inches.

iPhone 11 body ringside is made up of Aluminum as a result, it has a reduced weight of 194 grams/6.84 ounces.

iPhone 11 is prettily protected with a touch-sensitive *Ion-strengthened Glass.*

The Camera has two Rear (Back) Facing-Camera 12 MP while at the front of your iPhone one 12 MP Front Facing Camera is designed to take Selfie (i.e. yourself) with a 120° wide-angle Len.

The Camera screen display of your iPhone has Liquid Retina XDR Display of 1792 by 828 with 326ppi.

The iPhone 11 screen size is 154.9 Millimeters. It does not support Apple Pencil.

iPhone has IP68 Certification that ensures the safety of the use of the iPhone amid particles or dust and depth water.

iPhone 11 has a battery capacity of 3110mAh to serve you for 10 hours but it depends on the regular activities you are performing on it. If you are into a long-time hotspot or network data running activities regularly it may quickly rundown/discharge.

iPhone11 battery can be charged with a normal USB cable and adapter connector by plugging it into an electric socket.

Firstly put the small lightning connector end of the cable into your iPhone lightning port connector, the other USB end of the cord will be inserted into the USB port on the adapter and connect it to the power source.

More so, your iPhone came with a clear and sound ear pod that you can insert in the iPhone USB lightning port to receive or end calls, make requests from Siri, and hear an audio sound.

In the pack, you see SIM Tray Aiding-Ejector that will enable you to eject the SIM tray at the lower right side of your iPhone when you insert it into the pinhole and push the internal surface down to eject the SIM tray.

Turn the metal face of the SIM down and position the SIM according to the shape of the SIM compartment on designed on the tray.

iPhone 11 Pro Properties

The iPhone working efficiency is enhanced with 6 GB of *Apple A13 Biotic Chipset Random Access Memory.*

The iPhone internal memories range from 64 GB, 256 GB to 512 GB that also responsible for the iPhone price differences.

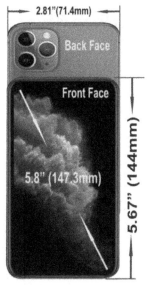

iPhone 11 Pro is produced with a thickness of 8.10mm or 0.32 inches.

iPhone 11 Pro body ringside is made up of a metallic ring with a weight of 188 grams/6.63 ounces.

iPhone 11 Pro is properly protected with a touch-sensitive *Ion-strengthened Glass*.

The Camera has three Rear (Back) Facing-Camera of 12 MP consist of two 12 Ultra Wide Camera and one 12 Telephoto Camera while at the front of your iPhone one 12 MP Front Facing Camera is designed to take Selfie (i.e. yourself) with 120° wide-angle Len.

The Camera screen display of your iPhone has Super Retina XDR Display of 2436 by 1125 pixel resolution with 458 PPI.

The length and breadth of the iPhone 11 Pro are 144mm or 5.67 inches by 71.4mm or 2.81inches.

The iPhone 11 Pro screen size is 147.3 Millimeters or 5.8 inches in diameter.

iPhone has IP68 Certification that ensures the safety of the use of the iPhone amid particles or dust and depth water.

iPhone 11 Pro has an internal rechargeable lithium-ion battery with a capacity of 3046mAh that will serve you for more than 60 hours when you are using for audio, above 17 hours for video replay, or above 10 hours for streamed video replay (playback).

You can charge the battery to half capacity within 30 minutes with an 18Watt fast lightning adapter. Besides, it can also be charged through Wireless charging functioning with Qi chargers.

iPhone 11 Pro Max Properties

The iPhone working efficiency is enhanced with 6 GB of *Apple A13 Biotic Chipset Random Access Memory.*

The iPhone internal memories range from 64 GB, 256 GB to 512 GB that also responsible for the iPhone price differences.

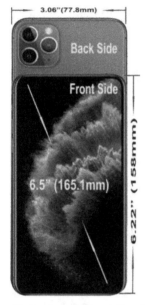

iPhone 11 Pro Max is produced with a thickness of 8.10mm or 0.32 inches. The length and breadth of the iPhone 11 Pro Max are 158mm or 6.22 inches by 77.8mm or 3.06.

iPhone 11 Pro Max body ringside is made up of metal steel with a weight of 226 grams/7.97 ounces.

iPhone 11 Pro Max is properly protected with a touch-sensitive *Ion-strengthened Glass.*

The Camera has three Rear (Back) Facing-Camera of 12 MP consist of two 12 Ultra Wide Camera and one 12 Telephoto Camera while at the front of your iPhone one 12 MP Front Facing Camera is designed to take Selfie (i.e. yourself) with 120° wide-angle Len.

The Camera screen display of your iPhone has Super Retina XDR Display of 2688 by 11242-pixel resolution with 458 PPI.

The iPhone 11 Pro Max screen size is 165.1 Millimeter or 6.5 Inches of Organic Light-Emitting Diode (OLED) in diagonal measurement.

iPhone has IP68 Certification that ensures the safety of the use of iPhone amid of particles or dust and 4 meters depth water for 30mins.

iPhone 11 Pro Max has an internal rechargeable lithium-ion battery with a capacity of 3969mAh that will serve you for more than 78 hours when you are playing audio, over 19 hours for video playback or more than 11 hours for streamed video replay (playback).

You can charge the battery to half capacity within 30 minutes with an 18Watt fast lightning adapter. Also, it can be charged through Wireless charging functioning with Qi chargers.

The iPhone in-build battery can be quickly charged with an 18W adapter.

Audio Playback Formats Accepted In iPhone 11, 11 Pro and 11 Pro Max

The iPhone can be used to play any audio sound produced in these formats:2, 3, 4 Audible Enhanced Audio, AAX, AAX+, Apple Lossless, AAC-LC, MP3, Dolby Plus of E-AC-3, Dolby Atom, FLAC, Protected AAC, Linear PCM, and Spatial Audio Playback,

Video Playback Formats Accepted In iPhone 11, 11 Pro and 11 Pro Max

The iPhone can be used to play any video produced in these formats: AirPlay Mirroring sent Video into Apple TV of 2nd Generation or later, Motion JPEG High Dynamic Range (HDR) with Dolby Vision, HDR10 products, MPEG-4 Part2, H.264, and HEVC.

You will need to buy the appropriate adapters that can be used to get 1080p on your iPhone.

1. Lightning to VGA
2. Lightning Digital AV Adapter.

You can buy the above quality adapters on Amazon marketing platform that is, *amazon.com*.

SIM to use

You cannot use a *micro-SIM card* on any of the iPhone, but you can use Dual SIM of eSIM and nano-SIM on any of the iPhone models.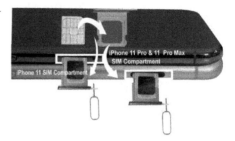

Cellular or Wireless to use on your iPhone

You can effectively use virtually all cellular or wireless models on your iPhone to connect to the network of the service provider. Ensure your SIM is registered and effectively activated for network function.

The Notch Part of the 3 iPhones

The Notch location is the top black center of your iPhone where there is Face Sensor, Stereo Speaker with Microphone, and Front-Facing Camera.

 Face Sensor: This recognizes the original owner's face that has captured and saved for Face ID during setup or later performed in the Settings. The sensor will be displaying blinking infrared light to scan your face to unlock your iPhone.

Stereo Speaker with In-Build Microphone: This will enable you to hear the audible sound and send voice sound to anyone calling you. It also helps during live-voice recording.

Front-Facing Camera: This is the camera designed to capture every image or object at the front of your iPhone screen including moving objects or living things like animals, plants, and humans. Therefore, you can use the Front-Facing Camera to take a personal picture called Selfie directly without asking any external support.

With Front-Facing Camera, you may time the capture and position the iPhone on a vertical stand to hold it for you and start your creative postures and admirable movement at the front of your iPhone. Once the time you set is elapsed/ended the camera will stop recording if you are using video but if you are using multiple shots the auto-shutter will stop. However, you will learn more in the later chapter for Camera Function.

Documents You Can Access on Your iPhone

There are documents you access on your iPhone 11, 11 Pro, or 11 Pro Max without looking for a format converter. Any of the accepted documents can be used or shared on the website page, mail, social media platform or to compose a message on your iPhone as a reminder or planner… and many others.

The documents are:

1. Microsoft Excel of XISX and XIS
2. Microsoft PowerPoint of PPTX
3. Microsoft Word of DOCX and DOC
4. Text of TXT
5. Image of JPG, GIF, TIFF;
6. USDZ Universal of USDZ, ZIP, and ICS
7. Keynote of KEY
8. Preview and Adobe Acrobat Document Format of PDF
9. Contact information of VCF
10. Rich Text Format or RTF
11. Numbers of NUMBERS format.
12. Web Pages of HTML and HTM

The iPhone Operating System (iOS) Version

The three iPhones have iOS 13 running in them which is the latest version of Apple iOS. This current version of iOS in your iPhone will enable you to benefit all the general invention and advancement on your iPhone if you carefully following all the problem-solving tips and techniques of using the different apps on your iPhone that are available in this book.

iPhone 11 Pro and 11 Pro Max Lightning Connection

The connection methods in iPhone 11 Pro and iPhone 11 Pro Max are the same because both iPhones are using the same type of fast USB connector to charge their batteries.

iPhone 11 Pro and iPhone 11 Pro Max are using 18Watt (W) USB-C Power Adapter with USB-C to Lightning Cable to charge approximately half of the battery level of iPhone 11 Pro Max and exact half of the battery of iPhone 11 Pro without power interruption.

The two-terminal connectors of the USB-C to Lightning Cable are small in size. One end of the cable is the same with one end of the iPhone 11 USB cable connector while the second end of the iPhone 11 Pro and 11 Pro Max is different from the other of iPhone 11 USG lightning cable as a result, I will show you the cable connection image.

GUIDE ONE

Moving Important Data from Old iPhone To New iPhone Manually

Important Notes

iPhone 11, 11 Pro and 11 Pro Max have many things in common that make their method of operation looking alike and completely the same in the term of setup, navigating apps (applications), many available apps, performing settings on your iPhone, the appearance of the individual page, operating menus/tools in editing, selecting tasks and movement from different app's pages to Home screen of your iPhone.

What makes their operation the same?

The mode of their operation is perfectly the same because iPhone 11, 11 Pro and 11 Pro Max are running with the same latest iOS 13 that display similar tactics of operating the various feature in all apps.

Development and easy approach in apps features are solely determined by the iOS running on a particular iPhone model as a result, the upgrading of old iOS in an iPhone to current iOS version will enable the iPhone to have new features and create access for the iPhone to perform all the function performed by the new iPhone model.

Therefore, most times it is advisable to update your iOS version to the latest iOS 13 that will only cost you cellular data and time sacrifice than buying a new iPhone model that would cost more.

For instance, if you are using iPhone X, XR, XS, XS Max running with iOS 12, all you need to do is to upgrade your iPhone iOS to the latest iOS 13 and subsequently enjoy all the benefits in the current iPhone.

However, you will always increase your iPhone storage memory to improve your iPhone's speed task execution but the efficiency of your iPhone can not meet 100% efficiency of iPhone 11, 11 Pro and 11 Pro Max because they are using advanced *Apple A13 Biotic Chipset Random Access Memory* that enhances the performance and execution speed.

If you are using preexisting iPhone models, that is, from iPhone 8 and below you can upgrade your iOS to iOS 11 – 12, then you will need to increase your storage memory perhaps your iPhone would be limited to perform some instant tasks and your mode of operation will remain the same but you will extensively benefit more.

Info: It is not all earlier iPhone models can work with either iOS 12 or iOS 13, please bear it in mind.

Tab 1: What are the differences in iPhone 11, 11 Pro and 11 Pro Max

Features	iPhone 11	iPhone 11 Pro	iPhone 11 Pro Max
XDR Display	154.9mm/6.1inches	147.3mm/5.8 inches	160mm/6.5 inches
Thickness	8.33mm	8.1mm	8.1mm
Side Ring	Aluminum	Metallic	Metallic
Weight	194g/6.84oz	188g/6.63oz	226g/7.97oz
Rear Camera	Two 12 MP Cameras, No Telephoto	Three 12 MP Cameras with Telephoto	Three 12 MP Cameras with Telephoto
Camera Resolution	1792 by 828 with 326ppi	2436 by 1125 with 458ppi	2688 by 1242 with 458ppi
Apple Pencil	Not Support	Not Support	Support
Battery	3110mAh	3046mAh	3969mAh
Battery	3hours more	4hours more	5hours more

Duration	than iPhone Xs	than iPhone Xs Max	than iPhone Xs Max
Adapter	Normal USB Charger	18W Fast Charger	18W Fast Charger
Cable	Lightning to USB Cable	Apple Lightning to USB-C Cable	Apple Lightning to USB-C Cable
IP68 Maximum Water Depth	2 meter for 30 minutes	4 meter for 30 minutes	4 meter for 30 minutes

What To Do First

What you must get ready before you start the manual processing of moving your important documents or data to your new iPhone.

- ✓ Charge your old & new iPhone battery to 100%
- ✓ Make cellular data available on your old iPhone
- ✓ Switch On Wi-Fi Network and Bluetooth on your old iPhone.
- ✓ Position the two iPhones vertically beside each other with a space of 2 to 3 cm between them.
- ✓ Insert functional Dual SIMs or nano-SIM (optional)
- ✓ Apple ID (optional)

Hindrance To Moving of Data Manually Through Setup

Correct the below conditions on our old iPhone before you start the manual setup:

- ✓ Off Bluetooth or Bad Rear Camera Sensor
- ✓ Poor Cellular connection or Wi-Fi Network
- ✓ Entering of Incorrect Apple ID
- ✓ Activation of "*Find My iPhone*" Settings.
- ✓ Low Charged Battery
- ✓ Low Storage Space (it make slow down the speed)

Starting Approach

You have been using a preexisting low iPhone model but now you want to move all your data and important documents into a new iPhone 11/11 Pro/11 Pro Max.

First things to do on your old iPhone are:

➢ Go to Control Center on your iPhone, tap on Cellular Service icon, Wi-Fi icon, and Bluetooth icon to turn them on.

 If the Wi-Fi network is not responding or you have not turned on Wi-Fi connection on your old iPhone before, then do the following step to activate your old iPhone **Personal Hotspot**.

Homescreen: Tap on Settings Button ⚙

Settings Page: Tap on Personal Hotspot

Hotspot Page:

1. Hit on **Personal Hotspot** activation switch ⚪ to turn green. ⚪
2. On a displayed Wi-Fi and Bluetooth are Off Box tap on **Turn On Wi-Fi and Bluetooth.**
3. On displayed Bluetooth Off Box tap on **Wi-Fi and USB Only.**
4. Hit on Wi-Fi Password

Wi-Fi Password:

1. Hit on the Password Text Field surface and use the keyboard below on the page to enter your **Wi-Fi Password**.
2. Hit on **Done** at the top angle of the iPhone.
3. Hit on Home button to return to Homescreen.
   But, if your old iPhone is iPhone X above then swipe up from the bottom.

Now that the old iPhone Wi-Fi Network, Cellular Service, and Bluetooth are turn on and active then you can move to the next stage of moving data from old iPhone to your new iPhone 11 or 11 Pro or 11 Pro Max.

Connect & Setup New iPhone to Start Working Immediately

1. **Power Switch Button**
   Look at the right side of the new iPhone you will see a button, Press down till you will see a big **Hello** font interpreting in different languages on the screen

2. **Hello**
   Swipe up from the bottom center to tap on your **Language**.

3. **Select Your Country or Region**
   Scroll down to tap on your **Country.**

4. **Quick Start**
   Look down the screen hit on **Set Up Manually.**

5. **Choose a Wi-Fi Network**

19

Hit on the name of your **Wi-Fi Source.**

6. Enter Password
   Enter the correct password of the **Wi-Fi Network** and tap
   on **Join** at the top right side of the screen.

7. Data & Privacy
   Hit the **Continue** bar

8. Face ID
   a. Hit on the **Continue** bar.
   b. Hit on **Get Started** bar
   c. Focus your eyes on the Front-Facing Camera Sensor
      and let your head be in the middle of the round frame
      on the screen.
   d. As you are turning your head gradually the surrounding
      lines of the round frame will be changing to green, keep
      turning your head and let every side of your head be
      captured by the Camera sensor till the surrounding lines
      are completely changed to green.
   e. If the Face ID is successful, a **Continue** page will
      display. Hit the **Continue** bar.

9. For later Face ID Settings hit the second option **Set Up
   Later in Settings.**

10. Create a Passcode
    Use the Keypad to type complex **Passcode.** But, if you are
    not prepared, then tap on **Passcode Options** and hit on
    Don't Use Passcode.

11. Passcode Box
    Hit on **Don't Use Passcode.**

12. Apps & Data
    If you are having data on Android Phone you can hit on the
    option **Move Data from Android. Other options**
    a. Restore from iCloud Backup

     b. Restore from Mac or PC

     c. Don't Transfer Apps & Data

13. Apple ID
     a. Tap on the Text Field, use the Keyboard to type your Email address
     b. Hit on **Next** at the top right angle side.
     c. Type a correct **Apple Password** inside the text field.
     d. Hit on **Next** at the top right angle side.

14. Apple ID Security
Hit **Continue** bar to register your **Phone Number.**
But, if do not want that to be done during setup then you tap on **Other Options**
Hit on **Don't Upgrade** on the **Request Box.**

15. Terms and Condition
Read through the terms and conditions that are required of you on how to successfully use your iPhone and follow them strictly. Tap on **Agree** option at the downright area of the screen.

16. Express Settings
Hit **Continue** bar below

17. Keep Your iPhone Up to Date
Choose the below option of **Install Update Manually.**

18. Apple Pay
Enter your Apple Wallet detail if it is available with you by hitting on **Continue** bar.
But, choose **Set Up Later in Wallet** option below, if you don't have.

19. Siri
Tap on **Continue** bar to register Siri (optional)
But, tap on **Set Up Later in Settings** to perform the full settings of Siri through the Settings process.

20. Screen Timer
    Hit **Continue** bar (optional), it could be done later, therefore, for now, choose **Set Up Later in Settings.**

21. Apple Analytics
    Select **Don't Share** option below Share with App Developers.

22. True Tone Display
    Hit on **Continue** bar

23. Appearance
    a. Select on **Light** option to make the iPhone screen appear brighter.
    b. Hit **Continue** bar

24. Display Zoom
    Hit **Standard** small circle to select it.
    Hit **Continue** bar

25. Go Home
    Hit **Continue** bar

26. Switch Between Recent Apps
    Hit **Continue** bar

27. Quickly Access Controls
    Hit **Continue** bar

28. Welcome to iPhone
    Swipe up from the bottom middle of the screen to access the **Homepage.** If you create a Passcode during setup, the iPhone will ask you to enter your registered Passcode before you can launch into the Homescreen.

Connect & Setup New iPhone to Start Working

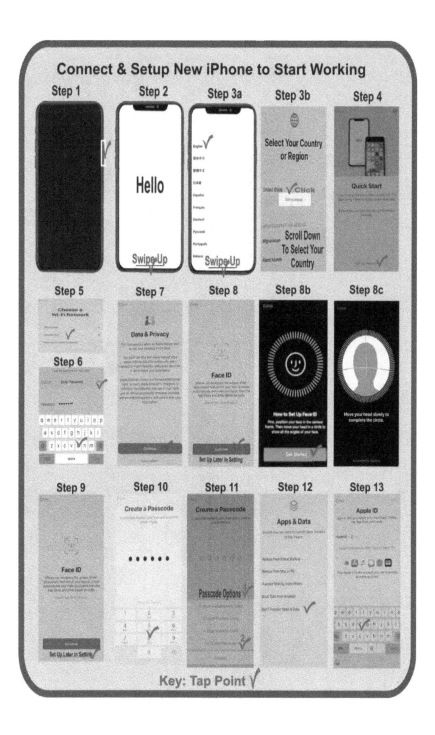

Key: Tap Point ✓

23

Connect & Setup New iPhone to Start Working

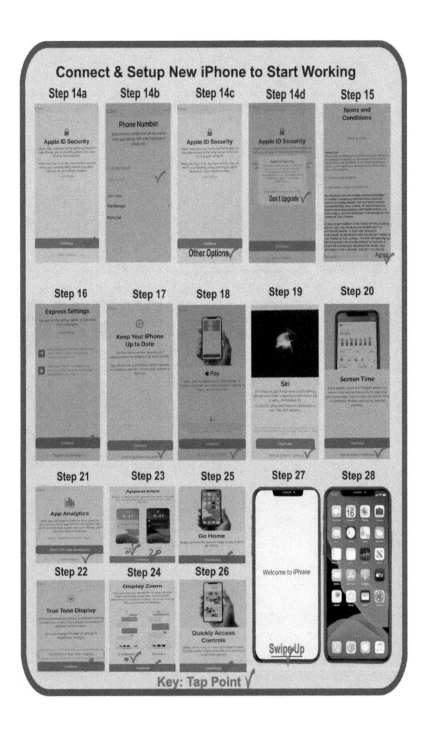

Step 14a **Step 14b** **Step 14c** **Step 14d** **Step 15**

Step 16 **Step 17** **Step 18** **Step 19** **Step 20**

Step 21 **Step 23** **Step 25** **Step 27** **Step 28**

Step 22 **Step 24** **Step 26**

Key: Tap Point √

Senior in Android Phone but Beginner in iPhone Operation to Move Data or Apps

As a beginner in the use of the iPhone, you need to upgrade all your previous data and apps on your Android phone.

- ✓ You should also make sure that your Android Phone Battery and iPhone Battery are 100% charged.
- ✓ Use a strong Wi-Fi Network and turn On your Bluetooth. Alternatively, you can initially do the manual setup of the new iPhone for you to use the new iPhone Hotspot Wi-Fi Connection on your Android to fast track the data or document transfer.

Take these steps on your old Android Phone

Homescreen

- ➤ Hit on Google Play Icon.

Google Play

- ➤ Hit on Google Play at the top of the page
- ➤ Use Keyboard to enter **Move to iOS** and tap on the suggested Move to iOS keyword dropdown.

Move to 1OS Interface

- ➤ Hit on **Open** bar
- ➤ Do not hit on **Continue** until you are on the page of Apps & Data where you will first hit on **Move Data from Android**

⇒ iOS Move from Android **on New iPhone**

- ➤ Hit on **Continue** below
- ➤ Type the **Code** that shows on the screen of your iPhone into your Android phone.

Move to iOS **(Pick Up Your Android Phone)**

- ➤ Hit on **Continue** above the phone image.

25

➢ Hit on **Agree**

➢ Hit on **Next** at the top angle the screen.

➢ Use the Keypad to enter the **Code** on the iPhone into your Android Phone.

If you have taken too much time before you enter the code into your Android Phone the transfer may be impossible.

If you experienced unsuccessful transfer, immediately, hit **Back** at the top left of the iPhone screen and re-tap on **Continue** to get another code. Enter the code fast into your Android Phone.

As soon as the transfer is complete on your new iPhone then tap on **Continue Setting Up iPhone.**

Continue your iPhone setup steps from Step 13 above to complete the iPhone setup.

Fast Automatic Approach to Move Data & Apps into New iPhone

Strictly follow all the instructions provided under "**What To Do First**" above before you start the fast automatic approach of moving data and apps into your new iPhone 11 or 11 Pro or 11 Pro Max.

How To Position Old iPhone and New iPhone

You can either position the old iPhone on the right side of the new iPhone or the left side of the new iPhone, but what is very important is that they should not be too far from each other.

26

If you are a lefty/left hand using a person you can position the new iPhone at the left side of the old iPhone.

But, if you are a righty/right hand using person, position the new iPhone at the right side of the old iPhone because you will perform more installation tasks on the new iPhone than the old iPhone.

Make sure that the distance is 2 to 3cm between each of them.

You may put your SIM card later but make sure the battery is 100% charged before you start.

In this cool guide, I used iPhone 6 with iOS 12.4 as my old iPhone. Any of the three iPhones (i.e. iPhone 11, 11 Pro, or 11 Pro Max) can be used as the new iPhone.

Hint: You must upgrade your old iPhone iOS to 12.4 above before you can successfully move data & apps to your new iPhone 11, 11 Pro, or 11 Pro Max that come with the latest version of iOS 13.

First Approach on Your Old iPhone

Save all your data with iCloud secure storage backup by navigating through:

Homescreen – Hit on the **Settings** icon

Settings – Hit on your **Name Profile**

Apple ID – Hit on **iCloud**

iCloud – Search downward and hit the **iCloud Backup** activation button to put on the iCloud Backup.

Backup – Hit on **Back Up Now** to start the iCloud Backup.

Home Button – Click on round Home Button down to go back to Homescreen immediately.

Start The New iPhone Automatic Set Up Approach

1. Positioning
   ➤ Place both old and new iPhone beside each other on a table.
2. Old iPhone
   ➤ Unlock the old iPhone and let it be on Homescreen.
3. New iPhone
   ➤ Press the switch button to "On" the new iPhone.
   ➤ Swipe up Hello, within a second your new iPhone will be seen on the screen of the old iPhone.
4. Set Up New iPhone **(Old iPhone)**
   ➤ Under the new iPhone's image hit the **Continue** bar.
   ➤ Within a second a round white shape Camera space will show up for you to capture the moving circular eruption.
   ➤ Take the old iPhone above the new iPhone, let the rear Camera focus on the moving circular

28

eruption, to be viewed in the center of the round space on the old iPhone above.

➤ Hold on till you will see **Finish on the New iPhone** on the old iPhone before you will return it to its formal position.

While the old iPhone is transferring the information into the new iPhone then go to the new iPhone to continue.

5. Enter Passcode of Other iPhone **(New iPhone)**

➤ Type Passcode of your old iPhone without making a mistake. Setting Up Your iPhone will show on the screen. Wait till you will see Face ID.

6. Face ID

➤ Hit on the **Continue** bar.

➤ Hit on **Get Started** bar

➤ Focus your eyes on the Front-Facing Camera Sensor and let your head be in the middle of the round frame on the screen.

➤ As you are turning your head gradually the surrounding lines of the round frame will be changing to green, keep turning your head and let every side of your head be captured by the Camera sensor till the surrounding lines are completely changed to green.

➤ If the first Face ID scanner is successful, hit on **Continue** bar and move your head in

29

either the same or opposite way, once the second Face ID scanner is complete another page will show and tell you that "**Face ID is Now Set-Up**"

➢ Hit on **Continue** bar

7. Face ID (If you do not want Face ID)

➢ For "later Face ID Settings" hit the second option **Set Up Later in Settings.**

8. Transfer Your Data

➢ Tap on **Transfer from iPhone.** If you have updated all your apps and data, you are good to go.

➢ You may also choose **Transfer from iCloud** if you are very sure that it is up to date. You may tap on **Other Options** to select any other device like Mac, PC, etc.

9. Terms and Condition
Read through the terms and conditions that are required of you on how to successfully use your iPhone and follow them strictly. Tap on **Agree** option at the downright area of the screen.

10. Settings From Other iPhone

➢ Hit on the **Continue** bar to proceed.

11. Keep Your iPhone Up to Date

➢ Choose the below option of **Install Update Manually.**

12. Apple Pay
Enter your Apple Wallet detail

30

if it is available with you by hitting on **Continue** bar.

But, choose **Set Up Later in Wallet** option below, if you don't have.

13. Apple Watch

➢ Tap on **Set Up Later** under the continue bar to proceed.

14. Apple Analytics

Select **Don't Share** option below Share with App Developers. The next interface will show you how the data is moving from your old iPhone to the new iPhone.

15. Old iPhone

When all the data are completely moved into your new iPhone 11/11 Pro/11 Pro Max, it will show on the interface of the old iPhone that "**Transfer Complete**".

Hit on **Continue** bar to enter the Homescreen of your old iPhone.

16. New iPhone

The New iPhone will show Apple's image on the screen. After a while, it

will change the screen face to a white interface. Swipe Up the screen from the bottom center and launch into the data loading Apple image interface of your new iPhone.

You have to endure enough to allow all the data and apps to absolutely moving from old iPhone to new iPhone because the uncompleted Apps will appear black with a faded icon image on the Homescreen. You will only see the icons that are completely loaded on your screen as they have appeared on your old iPhone.

GUIDE TWO

All The Important Security IDs You Need on Your New iPhone

Add Apple ID

Apple ID will protect your vital documents, Apple Pay Credit Card; it will enable you to buy more applications on your iPhone, create more lively activities, activation, or settings of different apps... and many others.

You need to have one iPhone ID to link all your Apple devices like Apple iPhones, iPads, Macbook, iMac, Mac, and Watch together. That is if you are privileged to have more than one same or different types of Apple's devices.

How To Create Your Apple ID Process

1. Homescreen Approach the Settings Icon by hitting on it.
2. Settings: Look at the side of Profile Picture at the top and hit on **Sign In to Your iPhone.**
3. Apple ID
   - ➤ In the Email text field, type your active **Email Address**.
   - ➤ Look at the top right angle of the screen to tap on **Next.**
   - ➤ Hit on an option of Don't Have An Apple ID
   - ➤ You will see an informative box with **Create Apple ID.** Tap on the option.
4. Date of Birth
   - ➤ Type in your **Date of Birth** in the provided text field.
   - ➤ At the top angle of the screen hit on **Next.**
5. Name: Provide your **Name and Last Name** into the text field and hit on **Next.**
6. Email

- ➢ Make sure you enter the initial **Email** without typographical mistake or choose to **Get Free iCloud Email Address** and hit on the **Next** option.
- ➢ If you choose **Free iCloud Email** tap on **Next** and **Continue.**

Password

- ➢ You will be allowed two times to type your **Password.** Type the same password in the first password text field into the second verify password text field. If incorrect it won't continue.
- ➢ Make eight and above digits of a password that can comprise of a number, uppercase, and lowercase alphabetical letters.
- ➢ Hit **Next** at the top to continue.

7. Phone Number

- ➢ Carefully choose your Country
- ➢ Type your **Phone Number** for your identity verification.

8. Verification Method: Select any of the below options:

- ➢ **Text Message**
- ➢ **Phone Call**
- ➢ Confirm your option with **Checkmark** and hit on **Next**

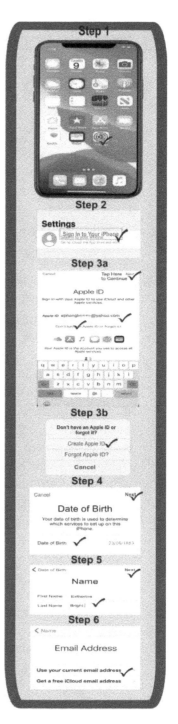

9. **Security Questions**

➢ Give an unforgettable answer to the security question you will be asked. You can write the question and the answer into your confidential organizer/planner to subsequently guide you in giving the exact answer whenever you are asked the same question during an essential activity on your iPhone.

10.

11. Verification Code

➢ Type the **Text 6-Digits Code** sent to you through your iPhone Message into the **Verification designated space** for the **Code.**

12. Terms and Conditions

➢ Read through the terms and conditions, digest, and get used to them or familiarize yourself to them because it is very important and hit on **Agree.** If you **Disagree,** that implies that you are not in support of Apple's Terms and Conditions guiding the Apple ID ownership as a result the Apple ID process will be discontinued /terminated.

13. Enter iPhone Passcode: Type your iPhone **Passcode** (4 or 6 digits). If you do not have a passcode, go to **Add Passcode** page on the section

to learn how to create your iPhone Passcode.

14. iCloud

➤ There will be a need for iCloud to get documents from Contact, Reminder, Notes, Calendar, and Safari on your iPhone. Therefore, hit on the **Merge** option.

➤ You may consider the other option of **Don't Merge** if you are having any otherwise opinion on their synchronization.

15. Find My iPhone Box

➤ On the box accept by tapping on **OK.**

Hint: You will see your Full Name appear where you saw Sign in to Your iPhone. Anytime you want to sign in to your iPhone hit on your Name and continue.

Now, you have created an Apple ID for yourself. Please you need to keep email & password details carefully to prevent false operators or fraudsters using your iPhone for illegal activities.

How To Change Your Apple ID Process

Homescreen: Approach the Settings Icon by hitting on it.

Settings: Look at the Profile Name beside Profile Picture at the top hit on **Name.**

Password & Security

➤ Hit on **Change Password**
➤ Type in your valid **Password.**
➤ Type in your **New Password**
➤ Type in your **New Password** again for confirmation
➤ Hit on **Change Password**

How To Sign In Apple ID On Your iPhone Process

Homescreen: Approach the Settings Icon by hitting on it.

Settings: Look at the Profile Name beside Profile Picture at the top hit on **Sign In to Your iPhone.**

Apple ID

> In the Email text field, type your active **Email Address**.
> Look at the top right angle of the screen to hit on **Next.**
  In the Password text field type in complex and easy to remember **Password.** Better still write it into your confidential organizer.
> Look at the top right angle of the screen to tap on **Next.**
> In the last part of the page, you will see Sign Out and hit on it to leave the page.

Now, you have added your Apple ID on your iPhone.

How To Recover Your Forgot Apple ID Process

Homescreen: Approach the **Settings Icon** by hitting on it.

Settings: Look at the Profile Name beside Profile Picture at the top hit on **Sign In to Your iPhone.**

Apple ID:

> First and foremost, type your correct Email add into the email text field.
> Look below you will see a 2-in-1 question state thus, Don't have an Apple ID or Forgot it?

- ➢ Hit on **Forgot it.**
- ➢ **On Informative Box** hit on **Forgot Apple ID.**
- ➢ Firstly, you will type in a new **Password** and secondly type the same password for the system to verify the correctness.
- ➢ Go to the top right angle of the screen to tap on **Next.**

You can verify it by tapping on Sign In, Type your submitted email, tap next, type your new approved Password and tap next.

Add Face ID

Face ID is another defensive mechanism/tool you can use to prevent fake users from using your iPhone. The use of Face ID on your iPhone will strongly enhance your iPhone security. It can be used to Unlock your iPhone.

You can use Face ID to buy things from iTunes Store, Apple Store, Apple Book with the use of your Apple pay.

Face ID in these modern developed iPhones (iPhone 11 or 11 Pro and 11 Pro Max) has replaced Touch ID in the lower iPhones, as a result, you will see Face ID & Passcode together under Settings on your new iPhone not Touch ID & Passcode.

But, it is less effective among the identical twins that are physically looking alike. It will be difficult for your iPhone Face ID infrared sensor to identify or differentiate the facially identical people.

How You Can Create Face ID via Settings Process

Homescreen: Approach the **Settings Icon** by hitting on it.

Settings: Search down to hit on **Set Up Face ID.**

Camera

- ➢ The Camera should be positioned in a portrait to capture your face. Don't allow any other person to stay behind you when you are taking your face.
- ➢ Hit on **Get Started** bar.
- ➢ Let your face be boldly covered in the Camera view center.

➢ Focus your eyes on the Front-Facing Camera Sensor and let your head be in the middle of the round frame on the screen.

➢ As you are turning your head gradually the surrounding lines of the round frame will be changing to green, keep turning your head and let every side of your head be captured by the Camera sensor till the surrounding lines are completely changed to green.

➢ If the first Face ID scanner is successful, hit on the **Continue** bar and turn your head in either the same or opposite way again, once the second Face ID scanner is complete, hit on **Done** bar.

Hint: If you are unable to turn your head or stiff neck, hit on **Accessibility.**

Add Passcode

Most of the time your iPhone will always ask you to create a personal Passcode to alternate Face ID to unlock your iPhone. In a situation that you are having an identical twin-face that the Face ID may compromise, you should have a Passcode that is only known to you, then you can use the Passcode to prevent your twin from accessing your iPhone without your consent.

In a situation whereby the Face ID failed to identify your face because of the face transformation you applied (i.e. face mask, excessive face makeup, etc.) then automatically your iPhone will request for your iPhone instead.

Surely, your iPhone will ask for Passcode anytime you perform the below tasks on your iPhone:

➢ For Installation of iOS
➢ Restarting or Switching On of Your iPhone.
➢ To Remove/Delete All The Data on Your iPhone.
➢ To Change or Access Passcode Settings on Your iPhone.
➢ To Perform Software Update.

38

How You Can Create Passcode via Settings Process

Homescreen: Approach the **Settings Icon** by hitting on it.

Settings: Search down the page and select the **Face ID & Passcode** option.

Face ID & Passcode

> ➤ Search down the page hit on **Turn Passcode On** option.
> ➤ By default, you will see 6 digits passcode which you can change to 4-digits passcode.
> ➤ But, if you are comfortable with the 6-digits type, then input complex **Passcode** that will have the mixture of Number, Small Case, and Capital Case of Alphabets.
> ➤ For 4-digits Passcode, hit on **Passcode Options** above the Keyboard and tap on the third option.
> > ✓ A Custom Alphanumeric Code
> > ✓ A Custom Numeric Code
> > ✓ **4-Digit Numeric Code**
> ➤ Re-type the complex Passcode for confirmation

Hint: You have to make your Passcode to be complex to prevent passcode hackers or guessers from predicting your passcode. Therefore, mix the passcode digits by selecting **Alphanumeric Code** and write it on your planner for record purposes.

Have you suspected that you present Passcode has been exposed to the wrong person?

Are you noticing suspicious operations on your iPhone?

Then, take a protective wise approach by changing the present passcode to a new Passcode.

How To Change Exposed Present Passcode Proces

Homescreen: Hit on **Settings Icon**.

Settings: Search down the page and select the **Face ID & Passcode** option.

Face ID & Passcode: Search down the page and hit on **Change Passcode** option.

Change Passcode:

➢ If you are using 6 or 4-Digits Password, type the insecure Password.
➢ The New Passcode will be requested to be re-typed twice.

Once you type the last digit, it will automatically approve and move to the previous page.

Activation of Apps in iCloud Account

The activation of apps in the iCloud account will determine the number of apps data that will be automatically uploaded and stored in iCloud storage for you to access them from all your devices. There are lots of suggested apps on your iPhone you can backup and store in the iCloud storage.

This can only be done if you switch on those apps on the iCloud page. Follow the below steps to select the appropriate apps that you want to back up with iCloud.

Therefore, you have to make more storage space available on your iPhone.

The example of the Apps is *Photo, Mail, Contacts, Calendars, Reminders, Notes, Messages, Safari, News, Stocks, Home, Health, Wallet, Game Center, and Siri.*

Homescreen: Approach the **Settings Icon** by hitting on it.

Settings: Look at the Profile Name beside Profile Picture at the top hit on **Sign In to Your iPhone.**

Apple ID: Look at the middle of the page and hit on the **iCloud** option.

iCloud: Hit the apps activation switch to change the switch look to green appearance.

Keychain:

> ➤ Hit on **Keychain** to turn "On" the **iCloud Keychain** switch.
> ➤ Return to the iCloud page by tapping on the **Back Arrow of iCloud** at the top left angle of the screen.

Hint: In all the devices you are using, it will constantly retain the credit card details and password you have accepted.

Find My iPhone

> ➤ Select **Find My iPhone** below the Keychain option under iCloud.
> ➤ Hit on **Find My iPhone** switch to activate it.
> ➤ Return to the iCloud page by tapping on the **Back Arrow of iCloud** at the top left angle of the screen.

Hint: This will enable you to locate, lock, activate, or erase your iPhone and other approved equipment if you produce your **Password**.

iCloud Backup

> ➤ Select **iCloud Backup** option
> ➤ Hit on **iCloud Backup** to activate the backup.
> ➤ Return to the iCloud page by tapping on the **Back Arrow of iCloud** at the top left angle of the screen.

iCloud Drive: It will accept all apps to store data and documents in iCloud.

> ➤ Hit on **iCloud Drive** to activate it.
> ➤ Move to the top left of the page to tap on the **Back icon** of Apple ID.
> ➤ Hit on the **Back icon** at the top of Settings and swipe up from the center bottom of the iPhone to go back to the Homescreen.

GUIDE THREE

Setup & Functions of Apps' Controls in Control Center

Control Center is a small page that contains all the essential apps icons that you can quickly access on either iPhone Lock-Screen or Homescreen.

There are lots of apps with their operational icons on your iPhone Settings that can be customized to be in Control Center for you to quickly access.

Primarily by default the following apps and operational icons are in your Control Center:

- ✓ Airplane Mode
- ✓ Cellular Service
- ✓ Wi-Fi Network
- ✓ Bluetooth
- ✓ Music Panel
- ✓ Screen Lock Rotation Icon
- ✓ Do Not Disturb
- ✓ Screen Mirroring Icon
- ✓ Screen Light Control (Contains True Tone & Night Shift)
- ✓ Volume Control
- ✓ Flash
- ✓ Timer
- ✓ Calculator
- ✓ Camera

Airplane Mode Icon: It is used to keep your iPhone out of cellular service or network activity when you are on the Airplane board. It is activated when you hit on the icon surface.

Cellular Service Icon: It is used to activate the cellular service network provided by your SIM cellular provider. Hit on the surface of the icon to see the name of the network provider and active bar at the top left of your iPhone.

Wi-Fi Network Icon: This is a network data-using service that could be activated through **Personal Hotspot** in the Settings or received from an external device like iPhone/Android, Mac, iPad, or PC hotspot via Wi-Fi connectivity.

Bluetooth Icon: This is used to receive or transfer any app data or document from, or to other Bluetooth supporting devices. Hit the surface of the icon to activate the function. You can use it to send sound from your iPhone to another **Bluetooth** supporting sound device to play the sound aloud. You can send one document at a time.

Music Panel: You can use this to play and regulate the sound volume of music from your *YouTube* or iPhone music sound. Hit on the surface of the *Play Panel* to control the sound.

Screen Lock Rotation: This will prevent your iPhone screen display to instantly move from portrait to landscape at any quick repositioning of the iPhone to the landscape. Hit the icon to permanent the portrait screen display but if you want to use your iPhone to watch the **video** you can re-tap the icon to deactivate the effect.

Do Not Disturb: You can use it to stop your iPhone from ringing, vibrating, and notifying you when you are in an important gathering, meeting, on the Airplane board, or driving a car.

Screen Mirroring Icon: This will enable you to see what is on the screen of your iPhone on your Mac, PC, Projector, or TV through the  use of a specific cable connector. Hit the surface of the icon to set the device connection and activate the application.

Screen Light Control: It is used to control the brightness and dimness of the screen light. If you want the screen light to be brighter, put your finger on the bright region of the control and move your finger up. But, if you want the screen face to look dim or dark move your finger from up to down.

When you press down the control **Night Shift** and **True Tone** will appear below the screen.

You can further change the mode to **Night Shift** mode that will change the screen appearance to yellowish-cream like the evening period to protect sight (eyes).

Although by default (i.e. from the factory) it is set to **True Tone**, the icon activation appears blue.

Volume Control: It is used to control ring tone, alarm, video, or audio sound volume on your iPhone. Place your finger on the surface of the volume icon and high the volume by moving up your finger or low the volume by moving down your finger.

Flash Icon: It is used to "On" **Touch/Flashlight** at the back of your iPhone. If you hit the **Flash icon** once immediately the Flashlight will display for you to see clearly or to make the back environment of your iPhone look like daylight and aids quick search.

Timer Icon: It is used to set various **Timer** formats and display the Timer on the **Homescreen.** Once you hit on the **Timer** icon you will access every detail of **Timer Setting.**

Calculator Icon: It is used for adding, dividing, subtracting, and multiplying numbers in mathematical calculations like mathematician, accountant, statistician, or everyone, and it can be extensively changed to a scientific calculator for a scientist to calculate advance calculation. Hit the **Calculator** icon for it to appear.

Camera Icon: It is quickly used to access a **Camera** page for you to take pictures and make videos. Tap on the Camera icon to get into the page instantly.

Add More of Apps' Controls in Control Center

Customize Apps into Control Center

Homescreen: Hit on **Settings Icon.**

Settings: Move down the page and hit on **Control Center**.

Control Center

- ➢ Hit on **Customize Control**.
- ➢ You will see **Access Within Apps**, put the activation button On if not activated by hitting on the activator.
- ➢ Hit on **Customize Control**.

Customize Control

- ➢ You will first see those controls that are in the Control Center listed above with a red circle having minus (remove) at the center that can be used to remove any of the controls from the Control Center if you deliberately hit on it.
- ➢ More listed Controls below are the available controls that you can add to those apps controls in the control center when you hit on the green circle having a cross sign (add) at the center. These are some of the controls you can add with those I have previously mentioned above:

Accessibility Shortcut, Apple TV Remote Alarm, Magnifier, Text Size, Note, Guide Access, Do Not Disturb While Driving,

45

 Low Power Mode,  Voice Mail,  Stopwatch… and many others.

➤ Keep tapping on the **Back** icon at the top-left region of the iPhone to return to Homescreen or **Swipe Up** from the bottom to return to Homescreen.

How To Confirm Your Customized Controls In Control Center

View Controls on Lock Screen or Homescreen

➤ Position your finger at the top right side of your iPhone and swipe down

You will see the additional controls below those controls I have mentioned above.

If you do not see it, go back to Settings again to confirm if the control is still among the list of **Add More.** If you see it among the list, then hit on the **Add Circle** at the front of the control Icon to add it.

If it is not among **Add More** but among the list of those that are already in control center then revisit the control center by swiping down the screen of the iPhone from the right side. Search carefully you will see it there.

46

Activate iPhone Screen Brightness from The Source

Homescreen: Hit on the **Settings Icon**.

Settings: Scroll down of the page to hit on **Display & Brightness** to access the settings.

Settings: Hit on the **Brightness** activation slide to become green.

> ➢ Slide the Brightness adjuster from left to right to elevate/high the screen light or you slide the adjuster from left to right to reduce the screen light.

GUIDE FOUR

Clew to All Fundamental Features

Avoid Ringtone, Vibration or Notification Distraction

There are two major ways on your iPhone that you can use to prevent calls from ringing out or to avoid vibration or notification alert or alarm sound.

External Buttons

Silent Mode Botton: This is the first small button on the left side of the iPhone that can be moved to the front and back direction of the iPhone.

When you move the small button from the front to the backside of the iPhone you will see red on the ground of the open and at the top of the screen will show notification of **Silent Mode On**. This means that you have muted the iPhone, therefore, there will be no sound from a call, alarm, and notifications but it will vibrate if you have previously activated vibration during settings.

But, when you move the button from back to the front of the iPhone the ring sound, alarm and notification alert sound will restore (i.e. unmute).

Do Not Disturb

Lock Screen or Homescreen: Swipe down the screen from the top right side of your iPhone notch.

Do Not Disturb Icon: Hit on the **Do Not Disturb** feature to prevent ringtone and vibration from any call, message notification, alarm, and alert sound.

How To Initially Put Do Not Disturb Into Action

You will perform this in Settings to make the feature to be effective on your iPhone.

Homescreen: Hit on the **Settings** icon

Settings: Search down for **Do Not Disturb** and select it.

Do Not Disturb: Hit on the activator button to change to green.

Schedule Time You Don't Want To Be Disturbed By Anyone

If you schedule the time you do not want people to disturb you with calls or messages then the above option (Do Not Disturb) will be deactivated automatically because you cannot use both features at the same time. You have to choose one.

Schedule: Hit on the Schedule, to set the time you don't want people to disturb you.

Specify Those Favorites That Your iPhone Can Allow

You have to choose some specific favorites that must be excluded from **Do Not Disturb** instruction. The **Favorite Contacts** maybe your Spouse, Children, Mother, Father, and Close Relative that may seek your attention unexpectedly should in case of any unforeseen Emergency.

Allow Calls From: Hit on **Allow Call From** to select your favorites by tapping on **Favorites** option.

Repeated Calls: Hit on the **Repeated Calls Activation Switch** to allow regular calls of your chosen favorites when you are busy till you pick it.

Activate: Hit on **Activate** to select **Manually** from the three available options which they are:

1. Automatically
2. When Connected to Car Bluetooth
3. **Manually**

Manually you will always be able to activate **Do Not Disturb** through Control Center.

Auto-Reply To: Select **Auto-Reply** to choose the **Favorites** and **Auto-Reply Message** that will describe what prevented from picking-up your iPhone presently.

Wake & Sleep Actions

The action will let your iPhone sleep and wake. If you are working on your iPhone and you quickly want to arrive at the **Lock Screen** without you making regular backing of pages to the page or swiping to Homescreen.

What you will do is for you to click the **Power/Switch Button** on the right side of the iPhone. Just a click the screen will go black meaning sleep and when you make a click again on the same **Power Button** the iPhone will awake at the **Lock Screen.**

Meanwhile, any of the security authentications like Face ID or Passcode may probably require. If your Face ID failed your Passcode will be automatically displayed for you to enter.

Auto-Sleep

Your iPhone may sleep automatically if the idle time (the time you are doing anything) has passed the time frame you set in the Settings of the iPhone screen activities, therefore, your iPhone will sleep. Wake the screen by clicking the **Switch Button** to wake it on the same page you have stopped working.

Lock Screen Beneficial Features

In the Lock screen, there are many quick activities you can perform to satisfy your need without moving into the Homescreen. The beneficial features are *Timer, Notifications, Touch, Camera, Apps, and News Searching Tool, Control Center, Padlock, Battery Charged Level, Network Strength Bar, Wi-Fi Indicator, and Cellular Service Provider's Name.*

The most important features you can work on and operate on them are:

Timer: It automatically syncs with the most accurate regional global time of your location. It instantly determines locational timing.

Notifications: It strictly works by your instruction to determine the information that will be shown on the Lock screen.

But, by default, it could display all information regarding calls, emails, messages, alerts, and alarm notification. However, you may restrict the exposure of your messages or mail detail from the Lock screen in the notification settings to prevent anyone from viewing your privacy.

You have to unlock your iPhone before you can be able to perform the following:

Flash: You can use the flash at the bottom left of the Lock screen to lightening the dark environment and facilitates sharp and clear output of pictures taking in uniformly dark surroundings.

Camera: It can be constantly used to perform video image capturing and pictures taking without you navigating through the Homescreen.

You could swipe from the right side of the iPhone to launch Camera page or press Switch button to access Camera and click on any of the down or up buttons for volume at the left side of the iPhone to take the shot if you don't want to use Shutter on the Camera interface.

Apps Searching Tool: When you slide your iPhone from the left side you will see searching tools that will enable you to find many apps information about your iPhone. Ask more of Apple store, iCloud or Siri to have full knowledge of them. There is much informative news that displaced below that you can hit on to read details.

Place your finger at the bottom of the Notch frame center of your iPhone and slightly move down your finger you will see a searching field with suggested favorite Apps that you can navigate to get what you need in the iPhone.

But, if that app you are looking for is not among the suggested apps, you can further type in the app into the searching field to access the app.

Hint: Whenever you see **Search or Text Field** on your iPhone without seeing any Keyboard to type text into the field. All you need to do is to initially hit on the surface of the **Search or Text field**, immediately Keyboard will appear below for you to enter your search text keywords into the field. Examples of apps that contain text field are Mail, Messages, Safari, or other Browsers, Camera, Call, Calendar, FaceTime… and many others.

Control Center: You can view Control Center from the Lock screen. Swipe down from the right side of the Notch at the center top of your iPhone.

Homescreen Beneficial Features

Virtually, all features available on Lock screen can be effectively performed on the Homescreen; even more can be done directly.

You can repeat the side screen and the Notch frame center searching methods on the Homescreen.

Several icons are available for you to navigate on to ease your smooth findings and operational functions. The individual app name is mentioned below as they were arranged row by row in the Homepage picture above.

This is the list of various applications (apps) that are available on your iPhone 11, 11 Pro or 11 Pro Max with iOS 13 are *Messages, Calendar, Photos, Camera, Weather, Clock, Maps, FaceTime, Notes, Reminder, Stocks, News, Home, iTune Store, Apple Store, Books, Health, Wallet, Settings, Podcast, Phone, Mail, Safari, Music, Find My, Shortcuts, Contacts, Compass, Measure, Calculator, Files, Watch, and Tips.*

You can still request more apps on your iPhone through Apple Store freely. More apps you can get from the Apple store are *iMovie, iTunes Remote, iTunes U, Number, GarageBand, Clips, Keynote, Pages, and Music Memos.*

All the above apps are very important for you to fully benefit the operational efficiency of your iPhone and make life very simple to

53

explore and achievable. **The most important and inevitable Apps that you must know the beneficial features are: Settings, Call, Messages, Camera, Photo, FaceTime, Siri, Safari, Mail, and Music.**

Settings: This app will enable you to access the settings of all the available apps on your iPhone. Through the Settings app, you can perfectly activate all the essential apps (e.g. Face ID, Siri, Passcode, Wi-Fi Network, iCloud, etc.) that you are unable or skipped during your iPhone setup.

Phone: This will enable you to reach out to your friends or loved ones that you are having their **contact** details on your iPhone. The phone app will enable you to receive and make a call.

Massage: This will enable you to send text messages to your loved ones in your contacts. You have two ways of sending a message to people.

1. SMS or MMS
2. iMessage

SMS or MMS: You can send a text message through SMS and MMS to anyone on your contact that is using an Android phone. The sending button is green

iMessage: This is a live interactive message medium that will enable you to see when the person you are sending your text message to is typing his/her messages. It is only available for those who are using an iPhone. The sending icon is blue.

Camera: This will enable you to take new pictures or images and record videos of any event. In it, there is image beatifying features that can be applied to edit and modify the image output.

Photos: In this app, you can fully access all your saved pictures regarding time, day, month, location, and event. This app will arrange and indicate the source of store images such as *Screenshot, WhatsApp, Facebook, Video, Movies, DCIM,*

Camera, Live Pictures...and others. You can add labels to any specific event photographs.

FaceTime: As the name of the app implies **FaceTime,** it will enable you to make face to face calls, audio calls, live chat text messages on your iPhone with the use of the latest Animoji or customized, Memoji and Emoji.

Siri: This app is a wonderful work-executor and apps, problem solver. It serves as a messenger or personal assistant to help you determine several activities associated with other apps on your iPhone. It can help you set and save time in Alarm, a reminder for events, check daily weather/climatic condition, recall the missed calls or messages and it can also help you compose messages and send to whosoever you want to send it to.

If you call its attention, it will do anything you want it to do for you. Its voice could be set to female or male voice all depends on your choice. It is one of the great successes ever apple has achieved in using technology to solve the iPhone user's bothering issues with ease.

How to talk to Siri

Safari: This app is used to browse for any information online or to download more applications, games, dictionaries, music, videos, language translator, WhatsApp, Facebook... and many others.

Mail: The App will enable you to instantly access your received email messages and to reply to messages.

Music: This app will enable you to play any audio music in your music library.

Now that you have familiarized yourself with all the essential Homescreen apps' icons and the most inevitable apps' features, then we have to move further on how you can apply their features and how to activate their functions through Settings.

How to Move App's Icons from a Place to Another on Homescreen

You can move any app on the Homescreen to anywhere you prefer it to be. You may choose to arrange the apps alphabetical order or base on the regular use of the apps.

Homescreen: For a short time press the screen for an optional box to appear.

Optional Box: Hit on the **Rearrange Apps** option. Immediate the entire apps will be stirring and unstable with the *Cancel sign* attached to the left top angle of each app.

Apps: Position your hand on each App you wanted to move and drag the app to the favorite place. As soon as, you are through with the rearranging of the Apps as you wanted then **Swipe Up** the screen from the bottom.

How to Keep More Than One Apps in a File on Homescreen

Homescreen: For a short time press the screen for an optional box to come up.

Optional Box: Hit on the **Rearrange Apps** option. Immediate the entire apps will be stirring and unstable with the *Cancel sign* attached to the left top angle of each app.

Apps: Position your hand on an App and drag it on another app to have the same file. Before you release the dragged App on the below App make sure that a transparent white square appears around the below app. You will see the File Name text field above, hit on the text field to name the file.

If you want more than 2 Apps in a file, then continue dragging Apps on the file you have created and hit on the external part of the file to restore and fix it.

As soon as, you are through with the rearranging of the Apps as you wanted then **Swipe Up** the screen from the bottom, the whole apps will come back to normal.

How to Return the Apps to the Previous Position

Created File

> - **Two Apps in a File**, hold-down the file for an optional box to show up for you to tap on **Rearrange Apps.** Immediately, the two Apps will be released from the file and show as an individual app on the Homescreen.
> - **More than Two Apps in a File,** hold-down the file to show an optional box for you to tap on **Rearrange Apps** and all the Apps will be liberated.
> - **If you want to be taken the Apps out of the file one after the other:**
>   - ✓ Hit the file compartment the whole Apps will be seen boldly.
>   - ✓ Place your finger on any of the App and drag it out. The file will contract back while the liberated App will be in its normal side.
> - **Swipe Up** from the bottom to stabilize the apps.

Delete Apps at the Homescreen

- ➢ Hold-down the app until you will see an optional dialog box.
- ➢ Hit on the **Delete** option. Immediately the app will be removed. *OR*
- ➢ Hold-down the app till you will see the whole app stirring and unstable with Cancel indication at the left angle the apps.
- ➢ Hit on the **Cancel sign**. Immediately the app will be removed from the page and the whole apps will automatically rearrange themselves.
- ➢ **Swipe Up** to stabilize the apps.

Choose More Attractive Wallpaper for Both Lock Screen & Home Screen

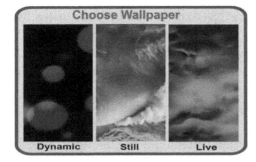

You can choose a beautifully attractive Wallpaper from various Apple-designed wallpapers or your admirable photo. The Wallpaper is sectioned into four categories:

1. Dynamic Wallpaper
2. Still Wallpaper
3. Live Wallpaper
4. Photo Wallpaper

Dynamic Wallpaper: The wallpaper contains several circular bubbles in different sizes that slightly increase in size on the screen.

Still Wallpaper: The wallpapers comprise of different designed stable images and natural picture without movement.

Live Wallpaper: The wallpaper shows movement when you touch the screen. Any image that is chosen in this category for your either Lock screen or Homescreen moves when you press down the screen. You can preview the animation before you set it for either Lock screen or Home screen.

Homescreen: Hit on the **Settings** icon.

Settings: Scroll down of the page and select (hit/tap) **Wallpaper**

Wallpaper: Above the Lock Screen and Homescreen Image hit on **Choose A New Wallpaper.**

Choose: You will see Dynamic, Still, and Live galleries in a row with the series of your photo events arranged in the column below.

> Hit on any of the Wallpaper options provided or your customized personal photo.
> Hit on a Set option below the **Wallpaper**. But, if you do not like it, you may select **Cancel** to take you back to Wallpaper Choose page to re-choose wallpaper.
> Optional Box will display three possible options that you may separately consider. There you can choose any of these options **Set Home Screen, Set Lock Screen,** or **Set Both.**
> **Set Home Screen:** The Wallpaper you have chosen will only appear on Home Screen.
> **Set Lock Screen:** The Wallpaper will only show on Lock Screen.
> **Set Both:** The Wallpaper will show in both Lock Screen and Home Screen. Therefore, you can choose two different Wallpapers for the two screens (i.e. Home & Lock Screens).

Homescreen Clever Tips

The Homescreen clever tips will prevent your iPhone from performing any of these malfunctions such as sudden sluggishness, jacking, irregular response to finger touch, or auto-switch off.

1. Always ensure that all the open pages on your iPhone had been completely closed on your iPhone before you sleep the iPhone.
2. Ensure your iPhone is fully charged before you use it to perform tasking activities.
3. Set low power mode on your iPhone to reduce the rate of energy consumption when battery capacity is 50 percent or less.
4. When the battery is low virtually the animation activation will be restricted (i.e. stop working) including the Live Wallpaper you have selected.

Complete Close of Opened Pages at the Homescreen

Homescreen to Lock Screen: Swipe down the left side of the Notch of your iPhone, alternatively place a finger at the center of the Notch bottom frame, and swipe down the screen toward the bottom of the iPhone. The Lock Screen will show.

How to Reduce Open Pages into the App icons on the Homescreen

Homescreen

➢ Hit on two-three different apps' icons on the Homescreen.
➢ Place your finger at the bottom center of the screen of the page.
➢ Slightly move up your finger for a small distance and take off your finger from the screen. You will see the app's page entering the app icon on the Homescreen.

How to See the Reduced Apps' Pages

Homescreen (Middle Screen Expose)

- ➤ Move up your finger from the bottom center of the iPhone screen and slightly move it in inverted seven Γ direction.
- ➤ As your finger is moving toward the right side of the iPhone you will see those open pages coming out from the left side of the screen.
- ➤ You can hit on any of the reduced opened app pages you still want to revisit to work on or get more information from.

Homescreen (Bottom Screen Expose)

- ➤ Place your finger on the first end of the horizontal line at the bottom center of the iPhone and move your finger to the second end of the parallel line.
- ➤ As you are moving the finger the page will be coming out one after the other. You can move from right to left or vice versa.
- ➤ Hit on any page you are looking for and it will fully display on the screen of the iPhone.

How to Remove the Reduced Apps' Pages

Page Pressing Down Method (after the exposed steps)

- ➤ When you press down the reduced open apps one by one for a while, they will show a **Remove Sign** of Minus a circle of red at the left top edge of their pages.
- ➤ Hit the **Remove** sign to complete delete the reduced page(s).

Swiping Method (after the exposed steps)

- ➤ Place a finger on the individual reduced open app and swipe up further to completely remove the page from the iPhone.

The complete removal of the reduced opened pages on your iPhone regularly will prevent your iPhone from a drastic slowdown of the iPhone speed efficiency.

Low Power Mode Battery Manager

The use of battery mode on your iPhone will enable you to use your averagely charged battery three times longer than usual battery strength.

When you have set the battery mode on your iPhone to be active at a 50% charged level of the battery, it will actively reduce many apps that are internally using the battery abnormally. However, the brightness of the screen light will be regulated according to the level of brightness you have set for **Low Power Mode** in the settings.

The Live Wallpaper will stop working when battery mode is active.

Activate Through Settings

Homescreen: Hit on the **Settings Icon.**

Settings: Move down the page to hit on **Battery**

Battery:

> ➤ Hit on the **Low Power Mode** to be activated by changing the button to Green.
> ➤ Go back to Homescreen by backing the pages or swiping up from the bottom center of the iPhone.

Activate Through Control Center

You can quickly activate the **Low Power Mode** Manually if you have customized the control through settings. If you want to know how to customize control, go to Guide Three and read how to **add more of apps' controls in the Control center**.

Homescreen/Lock Screen: Place your hand at the right side of the Notch above and swipe down to launch **Control Center.**

Control Center: Hit on **Low Power Mode** icon to activate the feature on the iPhone. The icon surrounding will change to white and the battery charge level will be yellow if it is activated.

Auto-Lock Battery Manager

Auto-lock comes to action immediately the idle time interval you have set has elapsed. That is, the iPhone will automatically lock itself after the seconds or minutes you have given to your iPhone to be active when you have stopped using it has passed.

In the Settings, you can instruct your iPhone to lock itself at any of this period below or you may even choose "Never" which is not helpful to the iPhone Battery.

- ➢ 30 Seconds
- ➢ 1–5 Minutes

Homescreen: Hit on **Settings Icon.**

Settings: Gently move down of the page to select on **Display & Brightness.**

Display & Brightness

- ➢ Hit on the **Brightness** activating switch to become Green.
- ➢ As you have activated the switch the Brightness regulator will be active. Then Move the Brightness regulator toward the left to reduce the light intensity.

Night Shift: If you have not activated the **Night Shift** hit on it and put it "ON". After you have activated it, go to the Control center to deactivate it by pressing down the **Screen Light Control** (Brightness control) and hit on **True Tone.**

Auto-Lock: Hit on the Auto-Lock to select your preferred time that you want your iPhone to remain active when you are doing anything.

Rise to Wake: Put "On" the activator, so that you may hit your iPhone screen when it is about to sleep.

Text Size: If you are not satisfied with the font size of the whole text on your iPhone you can go ahead and hit the **Text Size.** Move the Knob regulator toward the right to enlarge the text size on your iPhone screen. But, If, it is already too large, you can then move the knob regulator toward the left. (Optional)

Bold Text: You can make all the text on your iPhone screen to appear bold if you are not satisfied with the current look of the text font on your iPhone.

Hint: If you alter the text size or bold text, it will surely affect all the words on your iPhone.

GUIDE FIVE

How iTunes App Works

iTunes application is an important tool in terms of adding more pieces of stuff to your iPhone through your PC by sending and getting more pictures, music, video, etc. on your iPhone.

You can also use the iTunes Store to download many videos or music and play them offline on your iPhone with the use of a Wi-Fi connection. However, the service does not go free of charge, that is, you will pay for every music or audio requested at the iTunes store.

Syncing your iPhone with iTunes for more Lively Benefits

These are the following items you can add (sync) to iPhone from your iTunes library:

> Playlist,
> Movies
> Songs
> Podcasts
> Album
> Photo & Video
> Audiobooks
> Contact & Calendars

You should sync your iPhone with iTunes if you want to include the below items on your iPhone:

> **iTunes Playlists** but you will initially subscribe with **iTunes Match or Apple Music.**
> **Personal Video**
> **Calendars, Photos,** and **Contacts** provided you are not using **iCloud.**

65

You can also use iTunes to delete the formally added items from your iPhone.

All those lively benefits can be downloaded from the iTunes Store without you passing through the PC connection.

For you to get the iTunes Store App on your iPhone freely by using Password take the following step.

Homescreen

> Hit on **Settings Icon**

Settings: Hit on your Name or Sign In and select the **iTunes & App Store.**

iTunes & App Store: Hit on **Password Settings**

Password Settings

> Switch on Face ID for buying all you need.
> Below PURCHASE AND IN-APP PURCHASE hit on your desirable requirement (what you need).
> Below FREE DOWNLOAD you will see **Require Password**, hit the activator to become Green.
> As soon as, you are requested to provide your **Password,** then enter it.
> Hit on **OK.**

Get Video and Music from other iPhone to your iPhone

Settings on your iPhone and the other iPhone

Homescreen

> Go to **Control Center,** put On **Bluetooth** and tap the screen, or swipe up from the bottom center to go back to the Homepage.
> Hit on **Settings**

Settings: Select (tap) on **General**

General: Hit on **AirDrop**

AirDrop: Select **Everyone** and swipe up for Home or continually tapping on the **Back icon** at the top left of the screen till you get Home.

For iPhone Sending Video and Music (i.e. the iPhone Sending Video and Music)

Homescreen:

> ➢ **Videos**
>> ✓ Hit on **Photos Icon** to pick on a Video you want to select the video.
>> Or
> ➢ **Music**
>> ✓ Hit on **Music Icon** and select your preferred music.
> ➢ Hit on **Share Icon**
> ➢ Select **AirDrop** by tapping on it.

On Your iPhone

> ➢ Tap on **Accept** in the optional notification of **AirDrop.**

On iPhone Sending Video and Music

> ➢ Hit on your iPhone Name you are sending items to.

Instantly the new iPhone would receive the selected item.

Project Audio On AirPlay Speaker

Homescreen: Go to **Control Center**

Control Center: Hit on **Screen Mirroring** icon

Screen Mirroring: Press the **Audio Card** down for a few seconds and the **AirPlay** icon should be tapped on.

AirPlay Speaker: Hit the **AirPlay Speaker** to be connected.

Use Emergency Call to Prevent Unforeseen Danger

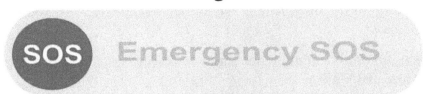

Get used to the instant ways of activating emergency provision and the quick approach of making the call when you noticed experience danger or around you that may result in loss of treasure or life if you do not get expert attention urgently.

Switch Button: Click the **Switch Button** 5 times.

Homescreen: Hit on the **Settings Icon.**

Settings: Move down to hit on **Emergency SOS**

Emergency SOS: Hit on **Also Works with 5 Clicks.**

Anytime you noticed sudden attack or unforeseen danger, all you need to do is just to click the Switch Button 5 times and instantly you will be connected to **Emergency SOS.**

Other Method

Press down **Switch Button** and **Up Volume** together for the **Emergency SOS** screen to show up.

At the center of the screen, you will see **SOS Switch.** Slide the **SOS** Switch from left to right side to be connected to Emergency Call.

Hint: You can also switch off your iPhone on the same page by moving **Power Switch** from left to right.

App Store Importance

You can fully download several apps and interactive social applications like Instagram, WhatsApp, Facebook, iMovie, Numbers, Keynote, Pages, GarageBand... and many others through the Apple store.

Homescreen: Hit on **App Store** icon

App Store: Hit on **Continue** bar.

Browsing Page: On a request optional box showing on your screen, tap on **Don't Allow** for Apple store not to access your location.

App Search: Look down the lower left side of the screen to hit on **Search Icon.**

> ➢ Hit the search field to type in your app request.
> ➢ As soon as you seen the App below, hit on **Get** at the opposite for instant **Download**.
> ➢ Make Home **Swipe Up** to see the new App Icon.

Notification Settings

Homescreen: Hit on the **Settings** icon.

Settings: Move down and hit on **Notification**

Notification: Hit on the **App Store**

App Store: Give commands to your iPhone by activating the provided options that are including **Allow Notification, Badge App, Show on Lock Screen, Show in History, and Show as Banner.**

> ➢ Hit on any of these options below:
>   > ✓ **Temporary Banner Show**
>   > ✓ **Persistent Banner Show**
> ➢ Make Home **Swipe Up.**

For Your iPhone Notification Preview

It is optional for you to choose where you want the notification preview to be shown when the iPhone is locked or unlocked. After the above steps, hit on the **Back** icon for Notification at the top left of the screen to return to **Notification Page.**

Notification: Select **Show Preview**

Show Preview: You may select **Always When Unlocked or Never.** But for confidentiality you may tap on **When Unlocked**, that means, it only you can see the notification(s).

Key to Protect your Cellular Data

This will enable you to reduce and control the rate at which all the cellular data-consuming apps on your iPhone would abnormally utilize your data within a short period.

Homescreen: Hit on the **Settings**

Settings: Select **Cellular**

Cellular: Opposite **Cellular Data** hit on **Roaming Off.**

Turn On the activation switch of **Low Data Mode** to green.

Rectify Freezing iPhone

Anytime you noticed that your iPhone suddenly stopped working by not responding to touch and opening of the app(s) is impossible then do the following of restarting the iPhone.

Stop working at any page you are on your iPhone

Left Side of the iPhone

> ➢ Click **Up-Volume** button
> ➢ Click the **Down-Volume** button.

Right Side of the iPhone

> ➢ Use 11 seconds to press the **Power Switch** button.

➤ The iPhone Switch Off and reboot itself to Lock Screen.

Lock Screen

➤ Home Swipe Up.
➤ Provide your **Passcode**
➤ Home Swipe Up.

GUIDE SIX

The Available Interactive Apps on Your iPhone

The applications (Apps) that have communication features on your iPhone will enable you to pass across information to people that are very essential to you and also receive information from them. The apps will give access to hear the live voice of your communicator(s) or recording conversation between them.

More so, through the communication app, you can make live text chat with your dearest fellows or colleagues or business partners or family and instantly receive a reply with the use of cellular data or subscription.

Above all, you can make conference audio or video calls with numerous of people. The Apps the have the **Communication Features** are:

1. Call App
2. FaceTime App
3. Message App
4. Mail App
5. Safari App

All You Can Do With Phone App

 Call app is one of the most essential primary cores of using the iPhone for communication. The use of Call App will enable you rich-out to your people of your through their phone numbers.

The people's phone number could be categorized into two places to separate the most important ones from general ones.

The most inevitable people are considered to be your **Favorites** on the iPhone while others belong to the general **Contacts.** You can assign a separate ringing tone to all contacts in **Favorites.**

By default, the Phone App is specifically positioned at the base bar of the Homescreen to ease your call making and receiving.

To save your friend contact in Phone app contacts, you will need the phone number, first and last name, email (if available), and picture (if available). But, it is very advisable to save your friend's email in the contact detail because you may need to reach him/her through your Email massage.

Add Contact

Homescreen: Hit on the **Phone App** at the base bar of your iPhone.

Source of Finding & Saving Contacts

Recents   Keypad
Favorites | Contacts | Voicemail

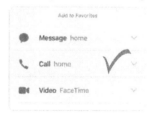

Favorites

> ➢ Hit on **Favorite** icon (Star) at the bottom left of the screen.
> ➢ Hit on **Add** icon (Cross) at the top left of your iPhone's screen.
> ➢ Go through all contact to locate the named contact or enter the name of the person into the **Search field** to quickly see the **Person's Contact.**
> ➢ Hit on the Contact Name
> **Optional Dialog Box:** Hit on the usual way of contacting people such as Message (iMessage or Mail), Call, or FaceTime. For example, select Call.
> Immediately, you will see the selected contact name among **Favorites.**

Add to Favorites
Message home
Call home
Video FaceTime

OR

Homescreen: Hit on the **Phone App** at the base bar of your iPhone.

Contacts

> ➢ Hit on **Contacts Icon** at the bottom center of the iPhone's screen.

- ➢ Hit on the **search field** to quickly locate the contact's name you are looking for.
- ➢ Hit on the contact's name to see all the person's information details, below you will see **Add to Favorites.**
- ➢ Hit on the Contact Name
  Optional Dialog Box: Hit on the usual way of contacting people such as Message (iMessage or Mail), Call, or FaceTime. For example, select Call.
- ➢ Immediately, you will see the selected contact name among **Favorites.**

Remove a Contact from Your iPhone

You need to understand the fact that, whenever you apply to **Delete** command on any contact on your iPhone or Email account, it will completely remove it from your iPhone without a chance of retrieving/restoring it.

Therefore, you have to fully sure about the contact before you hit on **Delete** command.

Homescreen: Hit on **Contacts Icon**

Contacts

- ➢ Search for the **Contact's Name** through the search field
- ➢ Hit on the exact **Contacts Name**
- ➢ Hit on **Edit**
- ➢ Move down the screen to hit on **Delete Contacts.**
- ➢ For confirmation re-tap on **Delete Contacts** (Confirmatory Dialog Box**).** Immediately the contact will be completely removed from your iPhone Contacts' list.

Set Sorting Order of Contacts List on Your iPhone

The Names of everyone in your Contacts could be arranged chronological order from A-Z to ease searching of either **First or Second Name.**

You are given the privilege to instruct your iPhone on how you want the name to be arranged, that is if you want the First name to appear before the second the following setting will enable it:

Homescreen: Hit on the **Settings Icon**

Settings: Scroll down to select **Contacts**

Contacts

> ➤ **Sort Order:** This will alphabetically arrange either the First or Second Name in Contacts.
> ➤ **Display Order**: This will either display the First Name after or before Second Name.

Short Name: Select how the Contact's Name of yours will show in Phone, Mail, Messages, FaceTime… and other Apps.

Move Contacts from SIM to iPhone

You can transfer all your contacts on your SIM into your new iPhone if the SIM supports the feature it is very easy to do.

SIM Card Insertion: Insert your SIM containing the contacts you want to transfer into your iPhone.

Homescreen: Hit on the **Settings Icon**

Settings: Hit on **Contacts**

Contacts:

> ➤ Move to the middle of the screen to hit on **Import SIM Contacts.**
> ➤ Hit where the contacts should be imported from an optional dialog box that will appear.
> ➤ Hold on till the whole contacts moving process finished before you proceed.
> ➤ Access your Contact to confirm the complete importation on iPhone.

Hints: iPhone cannot save the contact(s) on SIM card, if you want to transfer contacts from iPhone to iPhone then there will be a need for you to back-up the iPhone with iCloud storage or other transferring means like PC memory, flash, etc.

Activate and Deactivate Contacts for Mail Account

The activation of Contacts will enable you to add contacts in any of your Email Account and deactivation of Contacts will enable the removal of contact(s) from your iPhone.

Homescreen: Hit **Settings Icon**

Settings: Hit on **Password and Account**

Password and Account: Hit on the **Email Account.**

The Email Account (Gmail/Yahoo): Switch On the **Contacts Activator** to become Green.

To Deactivate Contacts App

The Email Account (Gmail/Yahoo)

> ➤ Switch Off the **Contacts Activator** to become **White.**
> ➤ Hit **Delete from My iPhone.** Immediately the contact will be removed.

Make Your Contacts for Email Account

Homescreen: Hit **Settings Icon**

Settings: Hit on **Password and Account**

Password and Account: Hit on **Add Account**

Add Account: Hit on your Email account and switch On **Contacts.**

If you do not have an email account you can hit on **Other** to make Contact Account such as LDAP or CardDAV account is available.

> Type your details and password.
> Hit on **Next.**

In a situation whereby you are having several accounts set up in the Contacts App and you actually need a particular account to have the contacts:

Homescreen: Hit on **Contacts** App

Contacts: Hit **Groups** at the top left angle of the screen.

Add New Contact to Your Default Account

This is very advisable for you if you are using more than one Email Account in your **Contacts.**

Homescreen: Hit on **Settings Icon**

Settings: Scroll down to select **Contacts**

Contacts: Hit on **Default Account**

Default Account: Select **One** of your **Email Accounts.**

Prompt Call Making

Homescreen: Hit on **Phone App**

Keypad Interface

> Type the **Contact Number** if you do not have the person's contact in your iPhone **Contact List.**
> Hit on the **Call Button.** It is the Green Circle.

End Call

> The Green Circle Button will change to Red Circle Button, it is called **End Button.**

➤ Hit the **End Button** to stop the call.

Make A Call from Contacts

Keypad Interface: Look at the bottom center to hit on **Contacts.**

Contacts:

➤ Enter the first-two alphabetical letter that started the name of the person into the search field to speed up the quick discovery of the contact.
➤ Hit on the **Contact's Name**

Contact's Name: Hit on the person's Phone Number.

End Call: Hit the **End Button** to stop the call.

Add People's Phone Number to Your Contact Directly

Keypad Interface

➤ Dial the **Phone Number** of the person correctly.
➤ Hit on **Add to Contact** at the top of the screen.

Request Dialog Box: On a displayed **Request Dialog Box** hit **Create New Contact.**

Create New Contact

➤ Type the First and Second Names
➤ Enter the Email of the owner of the Phone Number if you know it (optional).
➤ You can choose different **Ringtones** for the contact it is optional.
➤ Hit on **Add to Existing Contact**

Add to Existing Contact

➤ Look for the **Contact**

- ➢ Enter the Number into the Number text field
- ➢ Hit on **Done.**

Add To Contacts from Recent Called or Received Contacts

You can add the recently ended call phone number into your general Contact by following these steps on your iPhone.

Keypad Interface: Look below and hit **Recents** with a round clock icon.

Recent

- ➢ You will see the recently ended phone number
- ➢ Hit on the **Info Icon** in front of the phone number.

Info: Select **Create New Contact**

Create New Contact

- ➢ Type the First and Second Names
- ➢ Enter the Email of the owner of the Phone Number if you know it (optional).
- ➢ You can choose different **Ringtones** for the contact it is optional.
- ➢ Hit on **Add to Existing Contact**

Add to Existing Contact

- ➢ Look for the **Contact**
- ➢ Enter the Number into the Number text field
- ➢ Hit on **Done.**

Now the recent call will appear with the name you used in the adding of the number into your Contacts. The person contact can be found in your overall **Contacts list** on your iPhone.

How to Delete all Recent Contacts

A recent list comprises of the phone numbers of all those you have called, received calls and missed incoming calls, and missed outgoing calls with day and time they were called or received. You can easily remove all the recent history.

Homescreen: Hit on **Phone App Icon**

Keypad Interface: look at the bottom left of the screen and hit on **Recents** (Round Clock Icon).

Recents

- ➤ Look at the top left of the screen hit on **Clear**
- ➤ Hit on the **Clear All Recents** button showing down the screen. If you hit the **Cancel** button, it will reverse the action and the recent list will not be deleted.

What You Can Do When You Are On A Call

1. You can switch it to outside **Speaker**
2. You can switch to Video Call.
3. You can allow more people to your discussion.
4. You Mute the Voice.
5. You can Accept or Decline other incoming calls.
6. You can compose a message to reply to your call.
7. You can make use of Remind Me to program a remainder to later return the call of the caller.
8. You can search through apps (e.g. Mail, Photo, Note, Calendar, Safari, Social Media) to get relevant information. Browsing Apps will require a Wi-Fi network connection on your iPhone.

How to Allow or Prevent Call When You Are On A Call

To Accept Call: On the calling, the interface slides the Call button toward the right to answer the call.

To Prevent the Call and Forward It into Voicemail: Double-click the **Switch Button** at the right side of the iPhone.

Send Message To Caller: Hit on **Message Icon** to text messages and send them to your caller.

Use Reminder To Recall: You can hit on **Remind Me** to instruct reminding me to call the caller after you stop the current call.

Recalling of Forwarded Calls from Voicemail

Voicemail has a feature that can play your recorded voice greeting to tell the reason why you are not available to receive calls at the moment and also record and play the voice of the caller that audibly delivered messages for a very short time for you to hear.

You can also choose a greeting out of some default recorded greetings for your outgoing greeting.

To make Voicemail to be active you have to go into the Setting or through Voicemail Icon in the Phone app to Set Up your **Password and Greeting**.

Homescreen: Hit on the **Phone App** icon.

Keypad Interface: below the screen hit on **Voicemail Icon** at the last bottom left.

Voicemail: Hit on **Set Up Now.**

Password

> ➤ Type in the **Voicemail Password** that must be in 4-digit.
> ➤ Retype the same **Voicemail Password** to confirm your consistency.

Greeting

> ➤ Hit on **Custom** options to make your outgoing greeting with your voice or otherwise.

81

- ➢ Hit on **Record** to start. (Say your greeting as you want it to be said).
- ➢ Hit on **Stop** to end the recording.
- ➢ Hit on **Play** to hear your recorded greeting.
- ➢ If you are not okay, you can re-tap the **Record.**
- ➢ If you are okay then hit on **Save**

How to Reset Voicemail Set Up Through Settings

Homescreen: Hit on the **Settings icon.**

Settings: Select **Phone App**

Phone: Hit on **Change Voicemail Password**

Password

- ➢ Hit on **New Password**
- ➢ Type in the **Previous Password**
- ➢ Type in the **New Password**
- ➢ Hit on **Done.**

How to Listening to Your Voicemail

If you are having calls that have been forwarded into Voicemail, you will see the notification number of new Voicemails at the top- right edge side of the **Voicemail Icon** at the last bottom left of the keypad interface.

Homescreen: Hit on the **Phone App** icon.

Keypad Interface: below the screen hit on **Voicemail Icon** at the last bottom left.

Voicemail

- ➢ Hit on **Message**

- ➢ Hit on **Play** to hear the recorded caller's voice.

➢ Hit on **Call Back** to replay the voice message.
➢ If you are satisfied with the message you can hit on Delete.

To Call the Voicemail

Homescreen: Hit on the **Phone App** icon.

Keypad Interface: below the screen hit on **Voicemail Icon** at the last bottom left.

Voicemail:

➢ Hit on **Call Voicemail.**
➢ Hit on **End Button.**

Send Junk and Unwanted Callers into Voicemail

This is will only allow the saved contacts on your iPhone to ring-out but unknown contacts will be sent to Voicemail

Homescreen: Hit on the **Settings icon.**

Settings: Tap on **Phone**

Phone: Hit on the **Salience Unknown Caller** activator to become Green.

Set Call Waiting in Settings

Wi-Fi Network connection is very important to make Wi-Fi call active in Dual SIM. You will see Call Waiting when one line call is active and another incoming call occurs in another line.

Homescreen: Hit on **Settings**

Settings: Hit on **Phone App**

Phone: Select **Call Waiting** and hit on the activator to become Green.

➢ Make Home Swipe Up

Assign Ringtones to Calls, Alert, Mail & Messages

You can assign separate ringtones to different contacts in iPhone Contacts. You may consider giving similar ringtone and vibration to all the contacts in Favorite and different ringtones to some set of people in all Contacts.

You can use ringtone to know when closed family members in the Favorites are calling and when your important business partners are calling.

Homescreen: Hit on **Settings**

Settings: Hit on **Sound & Hepatics**

Sound & Hepatics

 - ➢ Hit on the **Vibrate on Ring** activator to turn Green
 - ➢ Hit on the **Vibrate on Silence** activator to turn Green
 - ➢ Select your **Ringtone** and choose any of the default Ringtones available.

Specific Ringtone for Individual Contact

Homescreen: Hit on **Contact App** icon

Contacts

 - ➢ Search for contact through the search field.
 - ➢ Hit on the **Contact**
 - ➢ Hit on **Edit**
 - ➢ Hit on **Ringtone**
 - ➢ Select one of the **Default Ringtones**.
 - ➢ Make **Home Swipe Up**.

GUIDE SEVEN

All You Can Do with FaceTime App

FaceTime App is an interactive method of communicating with those on your iPhone Contacts.

It has a unique video communication feature that can enable you to see the face of the person you are calling or the person that called you.

Most of the time, it is important that you first and foremost send a request to the person you want to make FaceTime video call with on either interactive iMessages interface or through an audio call that you will like to make or switch to FaceTime Video Call.

You have to ensure that the persons are using the iPhone and you are having enough Wi-Fi Data to make the call.

You can also use FaceTime to make Conference Video Call with other iPhone users in your contacts but you must notify those that will participate in the conference call on text message interface the time, the reason for the group discussion, and ask each of them if they will be available.

Make FaceTime Set Up in Settings to be Active

Homescreen: Hit on **Settings Icon**

Settings: Scroll down to select **FaceTime**

FaceTime

> ➤ Put On the **FaceTime** Activator to become Green
> ➤ Put On the **FaceTime Live Photo** Activator to become Green
> ➤ Provide your **Phone Number**
> ➤ Provide your **Apple ID**
> ➤ Provide your **Email Add** (Optional)

Make FaceTime Audio Calls or Video Call

Homescreen: Hit on **FaceTime Icon**

FaceTime: Hit on **Add Contact** at the top right of the screen.

Contact: Use the search field to quickly get the contact.

Audio Call: Hit on the **Audio Call button** to fix the audio call.

 OR

Video Call: Hit on the **Video Call button** to fix the video call.

How to Change from Normal Audio Calls to FaceTime Video Call

On the calling interface, you will see an option of using FaceTime Video

Video Call: Hit on the **Video Call button** to fix a video call.

Hit on the **End button** at the lower left of the FaceTime

Video call interface.

Change from Text Message Interaction to FaceTime Call

Homescreen: Hit on **Messages App Icon**

Message

> Hit on the **Compose icon** at the top right of the screen.

> Type the name of the person you want to chat with into the "**To**" Search field.

86

- During the live iMessage chatting with your friend, hit on the name of your friend at the top center of the screen to choose FaceTime.
- Hit on **FaceTime Icon**
- Choose either **Audio or Video Call**
- Hit on End button to end the FaceTime call

How to Make Multiple Chat

Homescreen: Hit on **Messages App Icon**

Messages

- Hit on the **Compose icon** at the top right of the screen.

- Type the **Names or Phone Number or Email Add** of all persons you want to chat with into the "**To**" Search field. For example, *Hannah Berm, Daniel Rose, Dan Floral*
- Below the screen hit the text message field for **Keyboard** to show-up, type your text message, and hit on **Send icon** to deliver your message into the chat interface.

How to Change the Group Conversation to FaceTime Video Call

It is the same step of moving from a single chat that you will take to change your discussion to FaceTime Video or Audio Call.

Message (Chatting Page)

- Hit on the names of your friends at the top center of the screen to choose **FaceTime**.
- Hit on **FaceTime Icon**
- Choose either **Audio or Video Call**
- Hit on End button to end the FaceTime call

How to Replace Your Face with Animoji during FaceTime Video

Homescreen: Launch **FaceTime** App

FaceTime

> On the FaceTime Call interface hit on **Video Call button.**

> Hit on **Effect Button.**

> Hit on either **Memoji** or **Animoji** available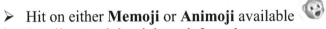

> Scroll toward the right or left to choose.

> Hit on your preferred Memoji or Animoji. Immediately your face will be replaced with chosen Memoji or Animoji.

> To remove the Memoji or Animoji hit on **Cancel** ✕ and your face reappear normally.

If you want to change the current Memoji or Animoji: Restart all over from the beginning of the above process and reselect the new Memoji of Animoji of your choice.

More of What You Can Do With Messages App

You can majorly use Messages App to make a direct live chat with those who are in your iPhone contacts using iPhone through iMessage.

Also, you can use it to send a text message to those who are in your contacts using Android.

How to Compose and Reply Text Messages

Homescreen: Hit on **Messages App Icon**

Messages

> Hit on the **Compose icon** at the upper right of the screen.

> Type the name of the person you want to chat with into the "**To**" Search field.
OR

> If you want to reply to any received message in the massage App, hit on the particular message. It will launch you into the compose text message interface.

> Hit the text field to type your text message.

➢ Hit the **Send Button,** that is, the Blue Send Button is for iMessage ⬆ while Green Send Button is for SMS⬆.

Your iPhone will automatically determine if the text message is iMessage or SMS. Once you see the blue button showing for sending your text message that implies you are about to send iMessage to the person using iPhone but if it shows green that means, you are sending text SMS to an Android user.

How to add Emoji to your Text Message

Messages

➢ At the lower left side of the Keyboard hit on **Emoji** Icon
➢ You may scroll up and down or right side to select by tapping on anyone you like.
➢ Hit on the Send button to move it into the chat interface.

How to add Effects to your Text Message

Messages

➢ At the immediate left side of the Keyboard Text Field, you will see **App Store** Icon, hit on it

➢ Select the **Animoji icon** at the bottom roll menu 🐵 .
➢ You will see different **Animoji** images.
➢ Select Animoji you like and position it within the square view guide. Once the Animoji is registered, it will be mimicking your face and mouth movement.
➢ Hit on **Recording Button** at the lower right side of the view frame to start recording your audio voice with Animoji. ◼
➢ Hit on the same button to stop the recording and ⬆ change the button to the **Send** button. It will replay itself for you to hear.
➢ If you are satisfied then hit on the **Send button** to forward the Animoji into the **Chat** interface for the person you are chatting with to receive and access.

89

➢ You can still reselect another Animoji below by scrolling through the arranged Animoji drawer and hit on another different Animoji to make a new recording.
➢ If you are not satisfied hit on the **Delete** button at the upper right.

For Additional Effects

➢ You can still go-ahead to get more Animoji in the App Store by tapping on the **App Store** icon at the lower-left corner of the screen and hit on **View Apps.**
➢ You can still search for **Images** that are very accurate to your message by tapping on **Search Icon** below.
➢ Hit on Find Images Field showing above the displayed images.
➢ Enter the types of images you are looking for like Thinking, Disagreement, Excitement, Sleeping, Busy, Hungry, Disturbed, Listening, Working... and many others. You may pick from the appearing keywords as you are entering the word.
➢ There is also a **Free Hand Drawing icon** that could allow you to draw anything you like and send it to the person you are chatting with.
➢ You can also send home videos through **YouTube, Audio Music, Recents Selfie Pictures/other Pictures, or Video** through Camera.

How to Make Memoji for Your Self

Messages

➢ At the immediate left side of the Keyboard Text Field, you will see **App Store** Icon, hit on it.
➢ Select the **Animoji icon** at the bottom roll menu .
➢ Scroll toward right hit on Add/Cross Sign for **New Memoji**
➢ Select **Skin** and adjust it with the available set of colors and remove face spots by choosing freckles.

- ➤ Select **Hairstyle** to choose either male hairstyle or female hairstyle
- ➤ Move to **Head Shape** to select the loveliest chin.
- ➤ Move to **Eye** section to pick the type of eye you like having on your Memoji.
- ➤ Continue to select all the parts of the face of your Memoji from the other options including **Browse, Nose & Lips, Ear** with different pretty earing, **Facial Hair** with either Mustard & Beard or Sideburns, **Eyewear** like glasses and **Headwear** like face-caps, hat, etc., till you complete achieve a beautiful looking Memoji. It is a creative place that is full of fun.
- ➤ As soon as you are satisfied with your **Self Making Memoji** then hit on **Done** to save the Memoji and include it with the group of Animoji.

You can use your Memoji to make FaceTime video call or iMessage audio chat on the Message App interface of your iPhone.

How to Add Animation Effect to Your Key Text Message

Messages

- ➤ Type your short text message into the text field. For example, *Stay Home Safe, Drink Responsibly, Daily Exercise Importance, Let's Jubilate, Today's Plan, etc.*
- ➤ Press down **Send** button for a while to launch **Effect Page** contains:
  - ✓ **Bubble Animation Effects:** Slam, Loud, Gentle and Invisible Ink.
  - ✓ **Screen Animation Effects:** Send with Echo, Send with Confetti, Send with Spotlight… and others.

Send with Effect

- ➤ At the upper center of the page, you will see **Bubble & Screen.**
- ➤ Hit one of the various effects menu to know the best. Once you have known the best leave it on the option.
- ➤ Hit on the **Screen** option above.

➤ Swipe the screen from right to left to see the various screen effects. When you have seen the most suitable **Screen Effect** for your Text message then hit on the **Send** button.
➤ If you are not satisfied then hit on the **Cancel** button to return to the message interface.

How to Send Voice Message

This makes the message easy to those who are not having enough time to chat or who are not very fast in a typing text message to quickly deliver their messages, as a result, they choose a short audio recording message that is précised, specific and facts.

Messages

➤ Go to the bottom left of the keyboard and hit on **Microphone Icon.**
➤ Start an audio message. You will see the linear sound wave of your voice as you are talking. The louder your voice the larger the width of the sound wave.
➤ As soon as you finished the audio message the hit **Send** button above.
➤ It will be seen in the chat interface.
➤ Look at the bottom left of the screen and hit on the Keyboard icon to return the Keyboard.

Hint: You can also dictate your message to Siri that is capable of changing all your audio dictation messages to text messages and sent it to the right contact you commanded.

More of What You Can Do With Mail App

 Mail app is an avenue to receive and send a message(s) with the use of Electronic Mail (Email) Service Providers which include **Google** (...@gmail.com), **Yahoo** (...@ yahoo.com), **iCloud** (...@icloud.com), **Outlook.com** (...@outlook.com)... and many others.

The use of the Mail App will fully allow you to receive or send documents to loved ones and business associates. It is more officially use for a better transaction between you and other business organizations.

Mail has become the most reliable acceptable official interactive platform to provide your vital details and execution of online obligation.

Therefore, the essential processes for you to become a wonderful beneficiary user of Mail great opportunities.

There are channels through which you can get information from that can be added to your composed message such addition is called **Document Attachment.**

You can save documents with any **Microsoft Office** formats or you may directly go to a website to copy very relevant information that is helpful to clarify your message and subsequently paste it within your message.

If you already have two more email accounts and you want to add them on your new iPhone there are some simple steps you have to do in your iPhone Settings.

To make Mail effectively functional, then you have to carry-out either manual or automatic set up in Settings on your iPhone.

How to Put Manual Set Up for Mail App in Place

The manual is simply designed for those who are using different Emails from the suggested email accounts on the Add Account Interface. Then, the **Other** is the correct option to choose.

Homescreen: Hit on the **Settings** icon.

Settings: Move down and select **Accounts & Passwords.**

Accounts & Passwords: Hit on **Add Account**

Add Account: Look at the lower region of the screen and hit on **Other.**

Other: Hit on **Add Mail Account**

New Account

> ➤ Type your **Name**
> ➤ Type your specific **Email Account**
> ➤ Type your **Password**
> ➤ Type your **Description**
> ➤ Hit on **Next** for the setup to be finalized and the Mail will search for your Email Account.
> ➤ Once the searching is successful then hit on **Done.**

If the Email Account Settings could not be found by Mail then do the following to roundup the setup.

Second Phase New Account: If you do not know your Email settings ask your email service provider to tell you if the email settings belong to IMAP or POP. As soon as, you confirm

> ➤ Hit on **IMAP/POP**
> ➤ Provide details on **INCOMING & OUTCOMING MAIL SERVER**
>   ✓ **Host Name**
>   ✓ **User Name** & **Password**
> ➤ Hit on **Next** at the top.

> Once your details are accurate then hit in **Save**

Your inability to provide the correct details will lead to the inability to complete the manual setup.

How to Put Automatic Set Up for Mail App in Place

Homescreen: Hit on the **Settings** icon.

Settings: Move down and select **Accounts & Passwords.**

Accounts & Passwords: Hit on **Add Account**

Add Account: Select your Email service source (e.g. Yahoo).

Yahoo

> Type your existing **Yahoo Address**
> Type correct **Password**

(If you want to look into your email account then you can hit on **Sign In**, when you are through, then **Sign Out** to return to the previous Set Up page because you still have some tasks to complete. Better still, complete the tasks before you Sign-In into your account).

> Hit on **Next** to continue and hold on for the processing to complete.

In Your Yahoo Account (...@yahoo.com)

> Switch On the **Activator** of the following applications **Contacts App, Mail Contacts, Calendar App, Note App & Reminder App.**
> Upper right region of the screen hit on **Save.**

How to Activate the Function of Essential Tools for Message Composition

All essential tools for a perfect write up and excellent message composition should be activated in the Settings to ensure correct spellings, arrangement, capitalization… and many others.

Homescreen: Hit on the **Settings icon**

Settings: Select **General**

General: Select **Keyboards**

Keyboards: Switch On the following **Activation buttons** of **Auto-Capitalization, Auto-Correction, Check Spelling, Enable Caps Lock, Predictive, Smart Punctuation, Character Preview, Shortcut and Enable Dictation.**

To Change Your Keyboard to One-Handed Keyboard

On the same Keyboards page

Keyboards: Select **One-Handed Keyboard** and hit on the **Activator**

OR

You can also get the selection of One-Handed Keyboard directly on the Mail to compose page.

Homescreen: Hit on **Mail App**

Mail: Hit **Compose Icon** at the top right region of the screen or select received email and later hit on compose or reply icon.

New Message

> ➤ Hit the front of "**To:**" for text cursor to show and the Keyboard to show below.

➢ At the lower region of the Keyboard in the new message interface, press down Earth icon 🌐 for different types of Keyboard to show.
➢ Hit on either left or right-hand side Keyboard that is very convenient for you.

How to Write and Send Email Messages

Homescreen: First and foremost, go to the **Control Center** to put On Wi-Fi Network and hit on **Mail App**

Mail: Hit Compose Icon at the top right region of the screen or select received email and later hit on compose or reply icon. ☑️

New Message

➢ Hit the front of "**To:**" for text cursor to show and the Keyboard to show below.
➢ Type the **Name or Email Address** of the receiving contact (the person's or company's email address).
➢ Hit the front of "**Subject:**" to type a short theme of your message.
➢ Hit on the text field interface to start writing your text message. Once you are through then hit on the **Send icon** at the top right region of the screen ⬆️.
➢ How to Directly Get Name or Email from Your iPhone Contact

You can directly get the name or email address of the person you want to send an email message to through the Contacts on your iPhone.

New Message: Hit on the **Add/Cross** icon to launch Contacts and use the search field to quickly locate the contact you are looking for.

How to Attach Document to Your Message

It is advisable to attach PDF or JPEG document on your Email because the document cannot be altered.

Mail: Hit Compose Icon at the top right region of the screen or

select received email and later hit on compose or reply icon. ⊡

New Message: After you have entered the above "**To**" info (name or email add of where you are sending a message), **Subject and** You have composed your message.

- ➤ Press down anywhere on the message field for **Edit Menu** to show.
- ➤ Hit on the **Arrow** at the end of the **Edit menu** to select **Add Attachment.**
- ➤ It will open to your iPhone document storage and iCloud Drive. Navigate through the App you used such as **Pages App, Keynotes App...** and others.

For Photo or Video

- ➤ You can also attach pictures to your message by tapping or press down the field and be tapping on arrow at the end till you will see **Insert Photo** or **Video.**
  - ✓ It will launch out your Photo library to select your **Pictures.** Carefully navigate through the exact category you have your pictures.
  - ✓ Hit on your **Pictures** and **Send** them to upload on your massage field.

Copy Information from Website

  - ✓ At the down middle of the iPhone Notch slide-down a little to see the App browsing text field.
  - ✓ Enter Safari, you will see the App and hit on it to access the web page.
  - ✓ Enter web add, highlight the massage, and hit copy.

- ✓ Go to the base of the horizontal bar and swipe from the left end to the right end. You will see the New Message page.
- ✓ Hit the place you want to paste the copied info to display on the message field for the edit menu to show an option of **Paste.** Hit Paste and what you copied will display.

OR

Homescreen: Hit on Safari to launch the web add text field.

- ✓ Copy your message as explained above.
- ✓ Move your finger from the middle bottom of the iPhone in inverted seven Γ to see the minimized **New Message Page**. (go to **Guide Four** learn "How to see reduced app pages")
- ✓ Hit on the New Message Page and follow the above pasting steps.

➢ Once you are through with all the documents attachment, then hit on **Send** ⬆.

More of What You Can Do with Siri App

Siri features will help you to organize and properly program your daily, weekly, monthly, and yearly activities successfully.

It is a unique tool iPhone that can help you to operate all the applications on your iPhone quickly and easily. Siri can help you activate any app or control on your iPhone.

Siri can supply you with all current information happening around the world; it could tell you the climatic condition as the moment, traffic condition, reminding you every important saved event in your organizer or calendar.

Siri could help you set alarm when you ask it to do so. It can change your dictated message to text message and send it to the instructed contact. It can translate the English language to any other language like French, German, Spanish… and more others.

It can help you locate a place on a Google map and show you the bearing compass to get the place. It can assist you to find out a review or reputation about an organization or person.

Siri can tell you where you can locate your favorites using iPhone that you have already registered with Siri. It could help you forward calls to your acquainted favorites or anyone in your contact… many other benefits.

When you call Siri, you will hear a human voice that could be a female or male voice. It depends on the types of sex voice you choose during Siri Setup.

However, for you to know all that Siri could do on your iPhone for you.

What to Do First with Siri

For Siri to work on your iPhone you must first and foremost finish the setup in the settings, if you have not done it during the iPhone Automatic Setup or Manual Setup.

Homescreen: Hit on **Settings**

Settings: Move down to select **Siri & Search**

Siri & Search: Put On all the below **Activation Buttons** and select your preferable features for each option.

> ➤ Listen for "Hey Siri".
> ➤ Press Side Button for Siri.
> ➤ Allow Siri When Locked.
> ➤ Language.
> ➤ Siri Voice.
> ➤ Voice Feedback.
> ➤ My Information.
> ➤ **SIRI SUGGESTIONS**
>   ✓ Suggestion in Search

✓ Suggestions in Lock Up

➤ Unlock the iPhone (If you did not activate " When Locked")
➤ Press the Switch, Sleep, or Wake Button at the right side of your iPhone. (If you have activated "Press Side Button for Siri")
➤ **Say**: Hey Siri! What can Siri do
  ➤ Siri will respond and show you all things that it could do.

 You can also use Apple Earpods to call the attention of Siri

➤ Click the Answering middle button to call Siri's attention.

Without Clicking on Side Button on Homescreen

➤ Say: Hey Siri!
➤ Immediately Siri will answer you. Siri is very sensitive to "Hey Siri", and then continue with your question.

All You Can Do with Safari App

Safari App on your iPhone makes use of Cellular Service and Wi-Fi Network Data to facilitate the efficiency, however, without network and data you cannot access Safari App.

The use of the Safari app will give the privilege of visiting many websites and move on a webpage to another webpage to gather several details or facts online.

Safari suggests a more related website that you can get more useful messages and also display all the favorite websites.

You can download or save apps through the Safari browser on your iPhone into My iPhone or iCloud drive. The Safari browsing window is loaded with many beneficial tools like:

➤ **Page Icon:** To move from webpage to another webpage 🗖

101

- ✓ **Add New Tab (Add Icon +)** to add more **Tab**
- ✓ **Private** to open a confidential browsing window.
- ✓ **Close Icon** to delete the page at the top left edge ✕
- ✓ **Done**
- ➤ **Share Icon** to send a page to other apps like Mail, Message, Add to Notes, Bookmark, Reading List, etc.; or to social media page which will be displayed the options of where you can save the webpage. Check any of the below options to determine what format the document will be sent:
  - ✓ **Automatic:** It will select the exact appropriate format for every application or action
  - ✓ **PDF**
  - ✓ **Web Archive**
- ➤ **Download Icon** to access the recent download files on Safari. ⊙
- ➤ **URL with A Small and A Big (AA):** Small A is used to reduce the font size and the big A is to increase the font size. It is designed to enable the following settings:
  - ✓ Small A Font Size Settings
  - ✓ Big A Size Settings
  - ✓ Show Reader View
  - ✓ Hide Toolbar ↖
  - ✓ Request Desktop Website 🖥
  - ✓ Website Settings ⊘

How to Put the Safari Settings in Place

Homepage: Hit on **Settings**.

Settings: Scroll down the screen and hit on **Safari**

Safari

- ➤ **SEARCH**
  Allow Safari to access Siri by tapping on **Siri & Search** and Activate the switch.
- ➤ **SEARCH**

- ✓ **Search Engine** will select your preferable source e.g. Google.
- ✓ Put On the **Searching Engine Suggestions** Activator.
- ✓ Put On the **Safari Suggestions** Activator.
- ✓ Hit on **Quick Website Search** to select **On**
- ✓ Put On the **Preload Top Hit** Activator.
- ➤ **GENERAL**
  - ✓ Activate **Autofill**
  - ✓ Put On the **Frequency Visited Sites** Activator.
  - ✓ Put On the **Favorite** Activator
  - ✓ Hit on **Favorites** to select **Favorites**
  - ✓ Put On the **Block Pop-up** Activator
  - ✓ Put On the **Show Link Previews** Activator
  - ✓ Hit on **Download** to select the storage source e.g. My iPhone and iCloud.
- ➤ **TABS**
  - ✓ Put On **Show Tab Bar** Activator
  - ✓ If you want Icons to be shown in the Tab then you may put On **Show Icons in Tabs'** activation button.
  - ✓ Hit on **Open Links** to select **In New Tab**
  - ✓ Hit on **Close Tabs** to select when you want the open tabs to be closed automatically by Safari. (e.g. Manually, After One Day, After One Week or After One Month).
- ➤ **PRIVACY & SECURITY**
  - ✓ Put On **Prevent Cross-Site Tracking** activator.
  - ✓ Do not activate **Block All Cookies** because they cannot transmit viruses and your iPhone details cannot be hacked by the network hackers.
  - ✓ Put On **Fraudulent Websites Warning's** activator
  - ✓ Put On **Check for Apple Pay** activator: it will enable you to if the Apple Pay activated and if you are having an Apple Account.
- ➤ **Clear History and Website Data:** If you hit this option you will be able to clear all the browsing history and website data on your iPhone.
- ➤ **SETTING FOR WEBSITE**

- ✓ Hit on **Page Zoom** for selection between 50%-300% but you may choose 100% for the normal setting.
- ✓ Hit on **Request Desktop Website** for selection of Websites.
- ✓ Hit on **Reader** for selection
- ✓ Hit on **Camera** for selection of Image Size.
- ✓ Hit on **Microphone** for selection

➢ **READING LIST**
- ✓ You can activate **Automatically Save Offline** if you want all reading lists in the iCloud to be automatically saved.
- ✓ Hit on **Advance** for selection.

How To Start Safari Browsing Benefit on Your iPhone

Homescreen: Hit on **Safari Icon** at the lower bar menu of the page.

Safari:

➢ Hit on the **Browsing Text Field** to type in your searching words from the appeared keyboard.
- ✓ You may select from the predictive dropdown keywords.
- ✓ You may also type your web address directly if you are very sure about it.

➢ Hit on the "**Go**" button on your keyboard and what you are looking for will come up.

If you are searching for social media applications like Facebook, WhatsApp... and many others then hit on the app or hit on download option if you want to download on your iPhone.

For **Webpage**: Once the page is displayed "you want to save the page as **Bookmark** for future or reference purpose".
- ✓ Hit on **Bookmark Icon** at the bottom of the page.

✓ Select **Add Bookmark for 3 Tabs** on the informative dialog box to **Save** it inside a **New Folder.**

✓ **New Folder:** Give the **Web Tab** a Name, hit on **Done** and it will be saved in the Favorite browsing tabs.

✓ If you want to open the web tab later. Hit on Bookmark and select the Name of the web tab and the page will open.

➤ **About Favorites:** These are the websites you visit often and automatically displayed below your Safari browsing search field.

✓ You can just hit on any of the come web icons to directly launch the webpage of the website without you retyping the website address into the search field machine.

✓ It is very easy and pretty cool to use.

✓ If still want to open another website, all you need to do is to hit on **Add New Tab** Icon at the right bottom of the screen. ╤

✓ A new page with your favorite websites will be displayed then hit on the other website to also launch another webpage for you to access easily.

➤ **Move From Tab Page To Tab Page**

✓ Hit on the Switch Page Icon at the last right bottom of the screen.

✓ You will see all the open pages filed up behind one another. With the help of your finger slightly swipe down to reselect any of the pages by tapping on the page.

✓ **Delete Tab Page:** Look at the top left edge of each page you will see **Cancel Icon**, tap on it and the tab page will be deleted.

➤ **Other Places You Can Save Your Place** ⬆

✓ Hit on the **Share Icon** to access the various apps that you can choose and save the web tap, as mentioned above.

➤ **Use Share Icon to Transfer Webpage from Your iPhone to Another Apple Device** ⬆️

✓ Go to the bottom of the page and hit on the **Share icon.**

✓ Select on **AirDrop** Icon

✓ Locate the Apple device **Name** and select. On the other Apple device hit **Accept** on the informative dialog box; instantly you will see the **Webpage** on the other Apple device screen.

When Webpage Could Not Be Loaded by Safari or Safari Not Responding

There are major technical problems that could prevent Safari from not responding or failed to load the webpage.

1. **Wi-Fi Network:** First and foremost ensure that there is an effective network of the Wi-Fi connection on your iPhone.

✓ **Problem 1:** If your Wi-Fi network is perfectly connected and there is no visible network indication on your iPhone.

✓ **Solution 1:** Relocate yourself to a place where you can see the Wi-Fi network because the stronger the Wi-Fi network the more Safari will be efficiently responding to the loading webpage.

How to Reactivate the Wi-Fi Network in Setting

Homescreen: Hit on **Settings Icon**

Settings: Select **Wi-Fi**

Wi-Fi: Put Off the **Wi-Fi** Activator 40secs and re-put it On. Go back to Settings and select **Mobile Data.**

Mobile Data: Put Off the **Mobile Data** Activator for a 40secs and re-put it On. Go back to Settings and select **General**

General: Select **Reset**

Reset

> ➤ Select **Reset Network Settings**
> ➤ Hit on the **Enter Password** that will show below.

Enter Password: Type in the **Password** and confirm the **Safari.**

Second Possible Problem

> ✓ **Problem 2:** If you are having s strong Wi-Fi network and Safari is not responding or loading a webpage.
> ✓ **Solution 2:** Crosscheck the Safari settings as some had been stated above and while the rest will be discussed below under **Settings.**
>
> 2. **Settings Crosschecking:** Initially go through all the Safari Settings above. Move a little further by tapping on **Advanced** to confirm the various activations Safari Settings.
> Homescreen: Hit on **Settings Icon**
> Settings: Scroll down to select **Safari**
> Safari: Start verifying the activated buttons one by one till you get to **Advanced**. Hit on the **Advanced.**
>
>> **Advanced:** Hit on each activation button to put Off and put On again. If you have not activated the below features on your iPhone before ensure that you activate them all because they are very important.
>> ✓ **Advanced:** Initially turn Off the feature one by one to confirm the Safari response, if it is working fine. But, if it is not yet responding put On the feature and repeat the same action on the next feature till you get the one that is responsible for the Safari abnormality.
>>> ▪ Re-put On the **JavaScript** activation button.

107

- Select **Experimental Features.**
✓ **Experimental WebKit Features**
  - Re-put On **Blank anchor target implies...** activation button.
  - Re-put On **Fetch API Request KeepAlive ...** activation button.
  - Re-put On **Quirk to prevent delayed initial pain...** activation button.
  - Re-put On **Intersection Observer...** activation button.
  - Re-put On **Media Capabilities Extensions** activation button.
  - Re-put On **Pointer Events** activation button.
  - Re-put On **Swap Processes on Cross-Site...** activation button.
  - Re-put On **Synthetic Editing Commands** activation button.
  - Re-put On **Block top-level redirects by third...** activation button.
  - Re-put On the **Visual Viewport API** activation button.
  - Re-put On **WebRTC H264 Simulcast** activation button.
  - Re-put On **WebRTC mDNS ICE Candidates** activation button.
  - Re-put On **WebRTC Unified Plan** activation button.
  - Re-put On the **WebRTC VP8** activation button.
  - Re-put On **Disable Web SQL** activation button.

GUIDE EIGHT

All You Can Do with Camera & Photo Apps

You can use the Camera app to access capture and take pictures of every image around you. The Camera is designed to take a live picture and modified compressed Panorama images. All the captured photographs are automatically saved in Photo Library.

In the Camera interface, you will see options that can be used to take different pictures and what you can do to add more attraction to the pictures.

The Camera can be used to take the photographs of anything including flowering plants, animals, human and nonliving things at the back and front of your iPhone by tapping on Camera rotating icon which "I called Camera Rotator" that can change the back facing Camera to front-facing Camera to take Selfie.

The different modes in your Camera are including Video, Time-Lapse, Slo-Mo, Pano (Panorama), Portrait, and Photo Mode.

To add more lovely effects to your picture, you can use Filter, Night Mode, Live Photo, and Burst.

What You Can See On the Camera Screen

1. Flash Icon: It is at the top left angle of the screen.
2. Night Mode Icon: It is located by the immediate side of the Flash.
3. Live Photo Icon: It is located at the right to the angle of the screen.
4. Edit Toolbar Menu Icon: It is located at the top center of the screen.
5. View Frame: It is located at the center of the screen where the image will appear.

6. Zoom Range: It is at the base of the View Frame to adjust the size of your image. -5x 1x 2x
7. Camera Modes in Row: It is at the top of the Shutter frame.
8. Thumbnail: It is at the left bottom of the screen to show a newly snapped image.
9. Shutter Button: It is at the bottom center of the screen to snap image(s). ○
10. Camera Rotator Icon: It is at the bottom right of the screen. ↻

There various ways you can access Camera on your iPhone.

Lock-Screen

➤ Slide your iPhone screen from the right side to left at the Lock-screen.
➤ Hit on the **Camera Icon** at the bottom right of the iPhone screen.

Homescreen

➤ Hit on the **Camera Icon**
➤ Position the Camera to pace the image at the center of the View Screen.
➤ Hit on Shutter or Up or Down Volume Button on the left side of your iPhone.

For You To Secure Your Photograph

Homescreen: Hit on **Setting Icon**

Settings: Select **Camera**

Camera: Select **Preserve Settings**

Preserve Settings: Put On the **Live Photo, Camera Mode,** and **Creative Control** Activators.

Zero Night Period

To prevent night defect on your photograph you have to make use of **Flash and Night Mode** Features to completely remove shadow or reflection of darkness on your picture outcome.

Look at the top left side of the Camera interface you will see Flash and Night mode of the screen; hit on the Flash to see select "ON" and also hit on Night Mode to change to yellow (ACTIVE appearance).

When you re-touch the Flash and Night Mode they will be UNACTIVE that is, they will stop working.

Night Mode: When you select the Night Mode a control will show to control the brightness of the image with time guide.

Photo Taking

You can take photos in a portrait by positioning your iPhone in the normal vertical position █ or landscape ▬ by making the iPhone to be positioned in a horizontal position (i.e. move the iPhone long side in 45° to ground level).

Homescreen: Hit on **Camera Icon**

Camera

> ➢ Hit on **PHOTO**
> ➢ Position the Camera either in Portrait or in Landscape.
> ➢ Let the image be at the center of Camera View.
> ➢ Hit the **Shutter** or click any of the Volume buttons at the side of your iPhone.
> ➢ You will see the photo in the **Thumbnail** below.
> ➢ Hit on the **Thumbnail** to review the Photo.
> ➢ You may also go to the Photo app to select your snapped picture.
> ➢ **To Delete:** Hit on Photo App and hit on all the pictures you want to delete and hit on **Waste Bin** at the bottom right of the screen.

Portrait Photo

It is an amazing invention of Photo modification the can make your Photo come out in various professional light to enhance the quality of the image.

The loaded lights are Natural, Studio, Contour, Stage, Stage Light Mono, and High-Key Light Mono respectively.

Camera Interface

> ➢ Look at the lower base of the View Frame scroll from either left to right or right to left to hit on **PORTRAIT.**
> ➢ Once you position your iPhone in Portrait the various light will show above the lower region of the View frame in arc direction.
> ➢ Hit the ball one by one to see its light effect on the image. Scroll toward the left to see the rest of the light.
> ➢ Let your image be either automatic focus (rectangular) at the center of the Viewfinder or hit any location on the screen to make your focus point.
> ➢ Hit on Shutter to snap the image. You can also do the same for yourself.

Pano Mode (Panorama)

Homescreen: Hit on **Camera Icon**

Camera Interface

> ➢ Look at the lower base of the View Frame scroll from either left to right or right to left to hit on **Pano.**
> ➢ First, let the Camera capture the left end of the image.
> ➢ View it in the rectangle Image View
> ➢ Hit on Shutter to start capture
> ➢ Slowly move your hand straight from the left edge side of the Image to the right edge side of the image. Use the Arrow on a straight line to guide your straight movement.
> ➢ Hit on the same Shutter to stop the shot.
> ➢ The Image will be spherically wide in size and look beautiful.

➤ You can also use it to make Selfies in the same method.

Live Photo

Homescreen: Hit on **Camera Icon**

➤ Look at the lower base of the View Frame scroll from either left to right or right to left to select **Photo**
➤ Hit on **Live** icon at the top right side of the Camera interface, the icon will change to yellow and you will see LIVE at the top center of the page.
➤ Let the Camera capture image correctly within a rectangle that is automatically showing at the center of the view fame.
➤ Hit on Shutter to take a shot of the image.
➤ The Image will be saved in the Photo library as Live Photo.

Zoom Capture

The Zoom sizes are shown at the lower base of the View Frame. If the image you want to capture is very small in the **Camera View** you can hit on either time 1 or times 2 to enlarge the image on your screen.

Finger Method

You can place your thumb and a finger on the screen and move them away from each other to enlarge the image or pitching screen to reduce the image. When you move the two fingers together it will reduce the image size.

Add Effect on a Saved Photo in the Library

➤ Camera Interface: Look at the bottom left of the Camera you will see a small rectangle show image, it is called **Thumbnail**.
➤ It the **Thumbnail** to view the recent image on the screen. Swipe from right to left to see more pictures you have shot before.
➤ Stop at the image you want to edit.

113

- Look at the top center you will see a menu minimized arrowhead which is called **Edit Menu** ⌃.
- Hit on the **Menu Toolbar** for a dropdown of different Edit options will appear.
- Select **Filter** and you will see the chosen image appear in different thumbnails with different color effects on each image replicate.
- Select the one like.
- Hit on **Done** to save the selected image.

Add Effect on the Captured Image

- **Camera Interface**: Look at the top center you will see a menu minimized arrowhead ⌃ which is called **Edit Menu.**
- Hit on the **Menu Toolbar** for a dropdown of different Edit options will appear.
- Select **Filter** and you will see different thumbnails with different color attractions. ◉
- Scroll from right to left and select any of the thumbnails with lovely color influence. The color will transform the image and the environment look.
- Hit on Shutter to take your shot.
- The newly captured image will be seen in the bottom left **Thumbnail**.

Use Burst Shot for Multiple Photo Shots at a Goal

It will enable you to take a continuous photo shot that you can later select the nice pictures among the total shots.

- **Camera Interface**: Let your iPhone Camera be positioned at the image.
- Use your finger to move the **Shutter** to the left without you lifting your finger till you complete all the number of **Burst Shots** you wanted to take at a time.
- The Camera will continually snap the image.
- Remove your finger from the Shutter, for it to return to the center and stop the continuous shots.

114

Video Recording

The Video mode is similar to Slo-Mo processes. The output of the Video will be accurate with the original movement without any delay.

To have the best of the Normal Video and Slo-Mo Video production on your iPhone with the highest quality resolution you have to initially do the following regulation in the Settings before you start the recording.

Homescreen: Hit on **Settings Icon**

Settings: Select **Camera**

Camera: Hit on **Record SLO-MO**

> **Record SLO-MO:** Select **1080p HD** at **240fps** (frame per second), return to **Camera** settings by hitting on **Back Icon** at the top left of the screen

Camera: Hit on **Record Video**

Record Video

> ➤ Select **4k at 60fps**.
> ➤ Hit on **Back Icon** to return to **Camera** settings.

Camera: Hit on **Format**

Format: Hit on **High Efficiency**

> ➤ Return to the **Homescreen.**

Homescreen: Hit on **Camera App Icon**

Camera Interface

> ➤ Select **Video** from the Camera Modes below View margin.
> ➤ Hit on the Red Recording Button to **Start** the recording.
> ➤ Hit on the button again to Stop the **Video Recording.**

Slo-Mo (Slow Motion)

You can apply motion with a timer to beautify modeling, sports activities, production stages, advertisement, growth... and many others.

Camera Interface: Below the View frame scroll the Camera mode and hit on **Slo-Mo.**

- ➢ Position your iPhone either in Portrait or Landscape the best way you want it.
- ➢ Hit on the Red Recording Button at the bottom center to start your either **Selfie Slo-Mo** or Scene/Event/Action taking place at the front of your Camera.
- ➢ Hit on the Red Recording Button again to Stop the **Slo-Mo Recording.**
- ➢ **To Play Your Recorded Slo-Mo:** Go to Homescreen and hit on **Photo App.**
- ➢ Hit on the Slo-Mo and it will play. You can share with your friends in iMessage, Social Media by tapping **Share Icon** at the bottom of the screen.

Thank you for buying this inevitable iPhone Guide companion. I strongly believe that at the end of the reading and application of all the working steps in this manual you would surely accomplish all your expectations and happy using one of the latest iPhone versions.

REFERENCE

SUPPORT.APPLE.COM/EN-US

www.ingramcontent.com/pod-product-compliance
Lightning Source LLC
LaVergne TN
LVHW041215050326
832903LV00021B/630